T3-BOE-523

LAW and Marriage

LAW and Marriage

F. A. R. CHAPMAN, M. A. (Laws) Cantab.

McGRAW-HILL

New York Toronto Montreal London
Sydney Johannesburg Mexico Panama

LAW and MARRIAGE

Library of Congress Catalog Card Number: 68-55595

1 2 3 4 5 6 7 8 9 10 THB—68 7 6 5 4 3 2 1 0 9 8

92499

Printed and Bound in Canada

CONTENTS

ACKNOWLEDGEMENTS

I am indebted to Dr. D. A. Barr, M.D., M.C.G.P., Director of Health Sciences at the Ryerson Polytechnical Institute, for patiently answering my questions on matters in this book which are of a medical nature.

I also wish to express my gratitude to Mr. J. A. Lennox Brown, LL.B. of the the Ontario Bar for having given me his valuable suggestions and advice on the topics of Succession, Estate Planning, and Taxation.

Neither of these gentlemen has been imposed upon to proofread the manuscript, so that any errors or inaccuracies in it are entirely my own responsibility.

On the other hand, if my wife did not check the authorities on the Etiquette of Divorced Persons with sufficient care, I am quite willing to let her take the blame. I just hope she will not divorce me as a consequence.

INTRODUCTION

One out of every two marriages ends in divorce in California; one out of every three in the United States ends the same way; and, one out of every fifteen ends similarly in Canada.

This relatively low divorce figure for Canada does not necessarily indicate that our marriages are so much more successful than those of our U.S. neighbours. Instead, the lower figure may be attributed to a reluctance toward divorce on moral considerations; because of religious prohibitions; or because of our laws, which have previously made it so difficult to obtain a divorce.

It will soon be established whether this last factor was the determining one. On July 2, 1968, the new Dominion-wide, Divorce Act came into effect, making the grounds for divorce in Canada much broader, and simplifying the procedure for obtaining a divorce. If the divorce rate does not rise significantly, it should indicate that we are a very well-married people. But, it probably will rise, for without a doubt, there have been innumerable couples waiting for this charter of liberty which now allows them to toss off the shackles of an intolerable marriage.

The main purpose in publishing a book of this nature at this time, is to acquaint the public in simple language with the details of this new legislation, constituting the first substantial change in almost 100 years. The new law, however, merely supplements the already existing matrimonial and divorce laws. Consequently, these are also explained. And, while we are about it, we will also discuss the laws of engagements and marriage which necessarily precede a divorce; and the laws of alimony, maintenance, and the custody of children which are the necessary corollaries to a dissolution of marriage.

We hope that the forthcoming ten chapters at least touch

upon, if not as thoroughly as a reference book for lawyers, all matters of a legal nature which might develop from the act of two people getting married.

This book is not designed to make do-it-yourself lawyers of its readers. However, we hope that it will draw attention to rights which people were not aware that they possessed against their marriage partners (to-be, present, or ex-) or against the world in general; and, that it will make them aware of the danger of entering into certain courses of conduct without, at least, first consulting their lawyers.

F. A. R. Chapman
Toronto, 1968

chapter 1

THE ENGAGEMENT

THE AGREEMENT

An agreement to marry between a man and a woman is an enforceable contract, provided all the other features and requirements which make a contract legally binding are present.

There must be an offer, the *proposal,* by one person (usually the man) to marry and an unconditional acceptance of that offer by the other person. This proposal must state clearly the offeror's intention to enter into marriage. Thus, when the vague young man says, "Darling, shall we get married or something?" his prospective mate makes the legal situation very clear by responding, "We'll get married or nothing."

If the lady waits too long before making her decision known to her suitor, he will be released from his obligation to her. All offers become void, *lapse,* if not accepted within a time which is reasonable under the circumstances; or, within a time which has been expressly specified for acceptance.

The agreement to marry need not be in writing in order to be enforceable; although a letter containing a proposal or a reference to the contemplated marriage will be better evidence of a disputed proposal than the jilted party's unsupported word.

Writing, however, is required to make enforceable any promise of a gift or a settlement which is made in connection with a marriage, such as a promise by the girl's father to provide a dowry.

If a man is introduced by a woman as her fiancé, and he does not dispute this designation while having an opportunity to do so, he is legally prevented, *estopped,* from denying the engagement at a later date.

Most contracts require consideration to make them binding; that is, something of value must be given in exchange for something received. You might ask where the consideration lies when a man promises to marry a woman, and to incur all the obligations connected therewith? The answer is that when a woman accepts a man's proposal, she gives him legal consideration by promising to marry him. In exchange, he gives his promise to marry her.

VOIDABLE AGREEMENTS

Contracts are not binding unless entered into voluntarily, of one's own free will. Consequently, a promise extracted by violence, or the threat of violence, is not binding; nor is a promise made while under the stupefying influence of drugs or liquor.

Many contracts entered into by people who are insane, or who are under twenty-one years of age, *minors* or *infants*, are voidable by them at their option; but not if the contracts involve the necessities of life, such as essential food, clothing, shelter, medical attention, etc. Marriage has **not** been held to be a necessity of this nature, and promises of marriage, therefore, are not legally binding on minors. It should be noted, however, that young people lose all such privileges and become adults for contractual purposes on the day preceding their twenty-first birthday.

And another field of law, called the law of *torts*, specifies that all thinking persons, regardless of their age, can be held responsible for certain losses which they have caused others by their improper behaviour (for example, fraud, negligence, etc.); legally, the person responsible must compensate for the damage done.

A promise by a married man to marry another woman after his wife's death, or after his divorce, is considered fundamentally immoral and is unenforceable. But such a promise by a man who had obtained a *decree nisi* of divorce was considered binding. (*See* page 95.)

GIFTS

Upon acceptance of his marriage proposal, a man often presents his fiancée with an engagement ring. Occasionally, couples may exchange engagement rings with each other, or other suitable gifts. A betrothal ceremony is not customary in Canada.

Should the couple wish to call off the engagement, they are free to do so since all contracts can be terminated by mutual consent. In such a case, engagement rings and other valuable gifts should be returned to the respective donors, since these gifts are regarded by law, not as outright gifts, but as *conditional gifts,* that is gifts conditional on a marriage ensuing. Gifts of a nature which might have normally been exchanged between friends need not be returned. In the case of a well-to-do couple, even quite expensive gifts might fall into this classification. It is also polite to return to the other person his or her photographs and letters.

BREACH OF PROMISE

If one person *jilts* the other, that is, breaks the engagement without adequate cause and without the other's consent, he is guilty of a breach of contract. False representations regarding one's finances, health, honesty, morals, potency, etc., are adequate causes for breaking off the engagement. Legally, the *jilter* can be held responsible for any loss which his improper behaviour has caused to the victim of the breach.

Breach of promise actions are rare today; in fact, they have never been as prevalent in Canada as they once were in England. Even there, they are dying out. Judges have long frowned on the blackmailing breach of promise actions instituted by designing women against men who often paid substantial amounts to settle an action rather than face the scandal of an appearance in court. Such a settlement, called a *mutual release,* should be drawn up by a lawyer for the full protection of both parties.

To collect damages, the jilted party must have suffered a loss, such as giving up her job, buying furniture, or becoming pregnant, in reliance on the promise of marriage. After a long engagement, a woman's lessened marriage eligibility can also merit compensation, although this factor is no longer of the same importance as it was in the days when a girl did not work for a living. The party who unjustifiably broke the engagement cannot be legally compelled to marry the other party.

The above are all rules of the Common Law and thus apply equally to all the provinces which derive their law from the English Common Law. They are substantially the same in Quebec and similarly apply to most of the United States.

chapter 2

GETTING MARRIED

The laws of marriage are similar in all the provinces. For the sake of convenience, the laws of Ontario are discussed first. Any important deviations from Ontario law by the other provinces are found at the end of this chapter.

MARRIAGE ACT

The laws of marriage in Ontario are governed by the Ontario Marriage Act of 1960 and subsequent amendments. According to its requirements, a couple wanting to get married must first either obtain a provincial marriage licence, have marriage banns published, or obtain a Special Permit from the Provincial Secretary.

LICENCES

Marriage licences are issued by city, town, village, or township clerks or their deputies in the local municipal office, if there is one. In the absence of these officials, a magistrate or properly appointed member of an Indian tribe or band may issue the licence. The licence fee is $10. This fee is waived in the case of Reserve or Crown land Indians.

To obtain a licence, a couple must accompany their application with an *affidavit,* a sworn statement testifying that no circumstances exist making them ineligible to marry; that is to say, they are not closely related and neither person is bound by any marriage ties at that moment. Only one person must swear to the affidavit if the birth certificate (or equivalent) of the other is produced.

No licence will be issued if the issuer doubts the validity

of the statements in the affidavit. However, such issuer has the power to take additional evidence from the applicants under oath, and then to issue the licence if he finds the additional information satisfactory.

The couple may get married three days after the issue of the licence; or sooner, if a Special Permit is obtained from the Provincial Secretary. The licence is valid for three months only, as is a Special Permit.

BANNS

Instead of procuring a marriage licence, a couple may have their respective churches publish the marriage banns according to the custom of the particular church. They may then get married within five days at the earliest, and three months at the latest, after the final banns are posted. Church banns are not available to persons whose previous marriage has been dissolved by divorce or annulment.

A licence will not be issued (except with the written authorization of the Provincial Secretary) nor will banns be published, unless at least one of the persons has had his usual dwelling place within the Province of Ontario for fifteen days immediately preceding the request for the licence or for publication of the banns, respectively.

SPECIAL PERMIT

The Provincial Secretary has absolute discretion to issue a Special Permit or to authorize the issue of a licence.

DISQUALIFICATIONS: BIGAMY AND INCEST

Some people are obviously disqualified from getting married. This is true when one is still married to somebody else, or if the couple intending to marry "stand within a prohibited degree of *consanguinity* (blood relationship) or *affinity* (legal relationship)". This means that one cannot legally marry anyone with a blood relationship which is closer than that of a first cousin.

For example, a man cannot marry his sister, his niece, or his granddaughter whether she be of the whole blood or of the half blood (that is related through both one's parents or only one) or by adoption; and, whether she is born legitimately or illegitimately. Nor can he marry any similarly close relative of his by marriage, for example, his deceased or divorced wife's daughter or granddaughter, or the widowed or divorced wife of his son, grandson or nephew.

The trick question, "May a man marry his widow's sister?" still catches many unwary victims. However, anyone in Canada may now marry his deceased wife's sister or niece. Until recently, some provinces (for example, British Columbia) did not extend this privilege to a divorced wife's sister or niece. There is nothing to prevent two brothers from marrying two sisters. If two disqualified persons marry one another, the marriage will be annulled and they may be prosecuted for having committed the crime of bigamy or incest. (*See* pages 43 and 46.)

PRESUMPTION OF DEATH

If a person's spouse has been continuously absent and unheard of and unheard from for seven years and no trace of his being alive is uncovered in spite of reasonable inquiries, a judge's order may be obtained declaring that such person may be presumed dead. When granted, this order has no further effect than permitting the other person to remarry. The "dead" person's property is not necessarily disposed of by such an order.

Should it develop later that the missing person was not actually dead at the time of the second marriage, the second marriage will become void. It will not be regarded as bigamous, although any children of it will be illegitimate in some provinces. In Ontario, as a result of the Legitimacy Act of 1962, they are legitimate.

By the Ontario Absentees Act, the court has the power to declare a person an *absentee* on similar grounds as previously discussed. Such a declaration will be made upon application by the absent person's kin or creditors. This declaration will be accompanied by the appointment of a trust company to act as the absentee's *committee*. This is essentially the same procedure as is adopted for a mentally incompetent person.

INCAPACITY

It is illegal to issue a marriage licence or a Special Permit to any person who is "mentally ill or mentally defective or who is under the influence of intoxicating liquor or narcotic drugs". It is also illegal for the marriage of any such person to be solemnized. Anyone knowingly performing either of these acts is punishable by a fine up to $500 and by imprisonment up to one year. Also punishable are people who issue licences and solemnize marriages without the proper authority; and, persons who knowingly make false statements in any documents required under the Marriage Act.

"Mentally ill or defective" signifies more than just having a low I.Q. It means the person in question has no proper realization of the transaction in which he is engaging. Similarly, being "under the influence" signifies more than having a drink or two to celebrate the forthcoming occasion. It means having one's senses so dulled as not to be aware of what is happening. In extreme cases, a marriage performed under these conditions can be annulled. (*See page* 46.)

PARENTAL CONSENT

Before a person under eighteen years of age can get married, his father's written consent generally must be obtained first. This requirement is subject to the following exceptions:

- The mother's consent is acceptable when the father is dead or when the father is living apart from the mother and is not contributing to the support of the child.
- When a guardian has been appointed, it is his consent that is required.
- No consent is required when: there is no guardian and both parents are either dead or have been declared mentally ill; the parents are resident outside Ontario, or are untraceable.
- When the person whose consent is needed, arbitrarily or unreasonably withholds his consent or when it is unclear who the competent person is, a judge may dispense with the consent upon receiving an application to that effect.
- In the case of a person under fourteen years of age, the consent must be accompanied by a certificate from a legally qualified medical practitioner to the effect that, without a marriage, an illegitimate birth would result.

MARRIAGE OF DIVORCED PERSONS

If a person has been divorced or has had his marriage annulled in Canada, a marriage licence will be issued to him only upon furnishing the original, or a certified copy, of the final divorce decree, judgment, or Private Act. If his divorce or annulment was granted outside Canada, he must first obtain written authorization to remarry from the Provincial Secretary. This will be granted after the submission of such satisfactory material as may be required. If such authorization is not granted, the couple either will have to forget about getting married, or they will have to move to, and get married in a country or state which recognizes the foreign divorce; even then the marriage may not be recognized in Canada if it can be proved that the couple left Canada for the express purpose of getting married. Otherwise, they will have to live Common Law.

COMMON LAW MARRIAGES

Living Common Law is often a euphemism, such as "living in sin", for any irregular union between a man and a woman. Lawyers, however, reserve this term for couples who have not gone through a regular marriage ceremony, yet live together permanently as husband and wife.

This is usually due to the fact that one (or both) of them has not been able to secure a divorce from his previous marriage partner. On the other hand, they may be nonconformists or want to take advantage of income tax deductions. For example, a successful businessman might be deterred from legally marrying a highly-paid employee, because her salary would no longer be an expense which is tax-deductible from his income.

In days past, common law marriages between competent parties had full legal status in remote regions, such as the Scottish Highlands. Going through a formal marriage ceremony there, was often coupled with considerable transportation difficulties. Even today, the common law partner of a war veteran has legal status in certain situations, and the Workmen's Compensation Act permits the payment of benefits to the common law spouse of a person accidentally killed at work.

SOLEMNIZATION OF MARRIAGE

The marriage ceremony can be performed by anyone ordained within a religious body (including Quakers) and properly registered to solemnize marriages. Some clergymen (Catholic Priests and Anglican Ministers in Canada) will not officiate at the marriage of a divorced person whose ex-spouse is still alive, except Anglican Ministers who may do so in quite unusual circumstances.

The marriage ceremony can also be performed by a judge or a magistrate in a *civil ceremony* between nine in the morning and five at night. His fee is $10. A clergyman is not entitled to a specific fee by the Marriage Act but he is customarily handed an envelope containing a cheque by the bridegroom's best man after the ceremony. Under international law, the ceremony can be performed in exceptional circumstances by any other authorized person, such as the captain of a ship on the high seas.

There must be two witnesses present in addition to the bride and groom and the person conducting the ceremony.

The marriage ceremony need follow no particular form, except that, at some part of the proceedings:

- Both parties must make a solemn declaration to the effect that they know of no lawful impediment to prevent the marriage.
- Each person must call upon the people present to witness that he takes the other to be his lawful wedded spouse.
- The officiator must pronounce the couple husband and wife.

After the ceremony, the officiator, the couple, and the witnesses must sign the marriage register and a Statement of Marriage. The latter had, previous to the ceremony, been endorsed on the licence (Special Permit or certificate of publication of banns) and been left with the officiator. On request, the couple is also entitled to a marriage certificate.

Marriage by Proxy. There is no marriage by proxy in Canada as there is in Argentina and some other countries. History records the marriage by proxy of some European princes. Even today, in one country, a girl can go through a form of marriage ceremony with the sword of her bridegroom who is away at war. Marriage by proxy was possible in the United States during World War II. In August 1968, a Washington,

D.C., judge married, by proxy, a Niagara Falls, Ontario, girl to a U.S. soldier who was in Viet Nam at the time.

Morganatic Marriages. By a morganatic marriage, the member of a royal family may marry a commoner without his children being entitled to inherit his rank or his estate however. Such a union is of a perfectly binding legal nature, and a morganatic wife must not be confused with a concubine.

IRREGULARITIES

If the parties to a marriage performed in good faith were not under any legal disqualifications (consanguinity or undissolved marriage ties) and have lived together after the ceremony as man and wife, such a marriage will be deemed valid in spite of any irregularities that might be revealed later. An irregularity might occur in the issue of the licence, Special Permit or in the publication of the banns; the person solemnizing the marriage may not be properly authorized to do so; the required parental consent may be lacking; or, there might be a violation of a requirement that is of a formal or technical nature only. None of these would affect the *bona fide* marriage. (*See* page 56 regarding the validity of foreign marriages.)

PROVINCIAL VARIATIONS

Alberta

Marriages may be performed by the clergy and by "marriage commissioners".

When the prospective bride or groom does not clearly understand the language in which the ceremony is conducted, an interpreter must be present and clearly explain the meaning of the ceremony.

Both persons must furnish medical certificates showing that a blood test reveals no syphilis. If this is not done, the marriage is declared **void.**

No licence is issued to a divorcé(e) for twenty-one days after the granting of a decree absolute and until it has become unappealable.

The court will declare an absent spouse presumed dead on

any reasonable grounds. His death is presumed automatically after a seven-year absence. For the presumption of death to be reversed, it must be disproven positively.

As in England, people under sixteen cannot get married unless the girl is about to, or has, become a mother.

Parental consent is required for the marriage of individuals under twenty-one, unless this requirement is waived on grounds similar to those of Ontario.

Between the ages of eighteen and twenty-one, the consent of one parent alone (that is, the father or a substitute, as in Ontario) suffices and even this can be omitted when the youngster has lived away from his parents for three months without their support.

Under eighteen, the consent of both parents is required. Without their consent, the marriage is void (if the couple have not yet had intercourse either before or after the ceremony).

British Columbia

The licence fee is $5.00; $1.00 for Indians.

After the issue of the licence, the three-day waiting period can be reduced by the Director of Vital Statistics for numerous valid reasons, such as an imminent pregnancy, a death, or one party having to leave unexpectedly.

Civil marriages can be contracted between ten in the morning and four in the afternoon, in a room with open doors.

Any person may pay $2.50 and lodge a *caveat*, a legal warning to the officials to suspend the issue of a licence until the person has had a chance to voice his objections. This will delay its issue until the facts have been satisfactorily investigated, or until the caveat has been withdrawn.

A satisfactory blood test is required.

Persons under sixteen cannot get married except with the consent contained in a judge's order.

The consent of both parents must first be obtained before a person under twenty-one (unless he is widowed) can marry.

Lack of a proper blood test or of the parental consent does not invalidate a marriage. However, there are punishments for the persons involved in violations of the legal requirements.

A remarriage ceremony is denied to couples who are still married validly to one another.

The British Columbia Marriage Act makes extensive provisions for Doukhobor marriages.

Manitoba

Licences may be issued between six a.m. and eleven p.m.

The marriage may take place twenty-four hours after the issue of the licence, or one week after publication of the banns.

The responsible clergyman may dispense with the banns at his discretion.

Marriage may be solemnized by a judge in his chambers with open doors between six a.m. and ten p.m. for a fee of $7.00.

Persons under sixteen cannot get married except to prevent an illegitimate birth.

The parental consent requirements are similar to Ontario except that no consent is required by a widow(er).

If there has been a violation of any of these requirements, the marriage is no longer voidable after one year, provided no absolute disqualification existed and provided the couple has cohabited.

Marriages can be performed in Manitoba for the residents of certain bordering areas in Saskatchewan.

New Brunswick

The marriage may take place at any time within three months following the issue of the licence which costs $5.50. However, a licence is not issued until five days after application.

The ceremony may take place five days after publication of the banns, or earlier, at the discretion of the clergyman.

A judge may perform the ceremony for a fee of $10.

A caveat can be issued for $3.00 as in British Columbia.

No minimum age requirement seems to be specified. Therefore, the English common law limitation of twelve years for girls and fourteen for boys would apply.

The parental consent requirements are substantially the same as those of Manitoba.

Marriages are not invalidated for the violation of technical requirements.

Newfoundland

Parental consent of both the parents is required for persons under twenty-one, except when the girl is about to, or has become a mother.

Marriages can be solemnized only by registered clergy within religious bodies, including the Salvation Army. However, magistrates and licenced laymen may perform the ceremony for women residing more than ten (sometimes fifteen) miles from the nearest clergyman.

Nova Scotia

A marriage licence is issued five days after application for a fee of $10.

The marriage can be solemnized by any member of the clergy or officer of the Salvation Army; or by a judge who may charge a $10 fee. (Until recently, it could only be solemnized by a male member of the clergy.)

The person officiating must wait three days (after receiving the names and other particulars of the couple to be married) before solemnizing the marriage, unless he feels an urgency exists.

Instead of signing the required documents, an illiterate party to a marriage may make his mark on them, properly witnessed.

Persons under sixteen cannot get married, except in the case of pregnancy.

The father's consent is required for the marriage of a person who is under twenty-one and not widowed.

A person who has married without parental consent while he was under eighteen can apply for an annulment before he reaches nineteen, provided there was no cohabitation.

Prince Edward Island

Marriage licences are issued one week after an application has been filed, for a fee of $3.25. A health certificate is also required.

To obtain a licence, a $500 bond must first be posted. This is forfeited if no marriage is possible due to a previous marriage or a prohibited degree of relationship. After the marriage has taken place, the bond becomes void.

The father's consent is required for the marriage of males under twenty-one and females under eighteen, unless they are widowed.

It is an offence, punishable by a $100 to $500 fine, to knowingly send a false marriage notice to a newspaper.

Quebec

Six months residence in the area in which the marriage is to take place is a prerequisite. If this is lacking, the marriage officer must ascertain that no impediments (consanguinity or previous marital ties) exist to prevent the marriage.

Only members of the clergy can solemnize a marriage in Quebec. The marriage must take place within one year after publication of the banns or the issue of the $20 licence.

An $800 bond must be posted for the same purpose as in Prince Edward Island.

The minimum age for marriage for men is fourteen and for women is twelve.

The consent of both parents is required for persons under twenty-one. If the two parents cannot agree, the consent of the father alone is sufficient.

In the case of a natural child, the consent of his *tutor* is required. An *emancipated minor* needs the consent of his *curator*. Before giving his consent, the curator must consult the minor's *family council*, composed of his relatives unto the fourth degree, that is, first cousins.

Under Quebec law a minor can be *emancipated*, or be considered of age, under certain circumstances. *Tutors* and *curators* are forms of guardians and trustees. (*See* page 27.)

Saskatchewan

Licences are issued five days after application for a fee of $5.00, between six a.m. and ten p.m.

The issuer must read the licence aloud to each person and supply an interpretation, if necessary.

The same requirement applies to the marriage ceremony which can be solemnized by a clergyman, or by a commissioner for a $5.00 fee, during the hours of six a.m. to ten p.m.

A medical certificate is required to attest to the absence of mental illness or a communicable disease.

Persons under fifteen (including Doukhobortsi) cannot get married except in the case of a pregnancy; which must be evidenced by a medical certificate.

The consent of both parents is required for the marriage of a person under twenty-one who is not widowed or divorced.

This consent is dispensed with if he is over eighteen and his parents are dead or insane, or if he has been living away from his parents, unsupported by them for three months.

A marriage will not be invalidated just because its form was irregular.

The Yukon and The North West Territories

The following are the almost identical Marriage Ordinances of the two Territories:

Licences may be issued between six a.m. and ten p.m. They cost $2.00 in the NWT and $3.00 in the Yukon. The licence application must be read aloud to the couple and when necessary, be explained to them and/or interpreted for them.

The marriage must take place within three months after the issue of the licence or the publication of the banns. In the Yukon, there is a twenty-four hour waiting period after the licence has been issued before the ceremony can take place.

Persons under fifteen years of age cannot get married unless pregnant, or with the written permission of The Commissioner who is the head of the government in the Territories.

The consent of both parents is required for the marriage of a person under twenty-one, subject to the usual exceptions.

Further, consent is excused for a person over eighteen who has been living away from his parents, unsupported by them for six months, or who has been living in the Territories for twelve months while his parents lived elsewhere.

A judge has the power to order an absent person presumed dead on any reasonable grounds, at any time. After an absence of seven years, no particular further grounds need to be adduced.

Marriages can be performed by clergymen or by marriage commissioners (not to be confused with The Commissioner).

Every Justice of Peace who has been given the powers of two Justices is an ex-officio marriage commissioner. The fee for his services is $5.00.

The ceremony must be performed between six a.m. and ten p.m. before two witnesses. It is illegal to marry lunatics, the carriers of a communicable disease in a communicable condition, or persons under the influence of alcohol.

A lack of the prescribed formalities and consent does not invalidate a marriage.

chapter 3

THE MARRIAGE

At one time, man took unto himself a wife by snatching her from a neighbouring village or by purchasing her from her father. The better her qualifications and the more desirable her qualities, the higher was the price. With the advent of Christianity, the Canon Law of the Church (upon which our present-day matrimonial and succession laws are founded) placed marriage upon a different basis. It regards the union of a man and woman as a form of contract, whereby each person assumes certain responsibilities and obtains certain rights. To the exclusion of all others, it is a union between them for life.

The Common Law does not spell out the terms of this contract specifically. The wording of the religious marriage ceremonies is not uniform either, although in the traditional ceremony the couple promise "to love, cherish, honour (and sometimes, to obey) one another for better or worse, for richer or for poorer, in sickness and in health, until death do them part."

On marriage, a woman takes on her husband's name. If this custom conflicts with her feminist principles, she and her husband can get married in a territory such as Gibraltar where women can retain their maiden names after marriage.

A wife can have a passport of her own; it is also possible for the couple to have one passport which covers both of them.

FAMILY RESPONSIBILITIES

The Quebec Civil Code makes the following specific requirements an implied part of every marriage contract:

- Spouses owe each other "fidelity, succor, and assistance".
- The husband must supply the family with the necessities of life.

- The husband and the wife are to be jointly in moral and material control of the family and its maintenance and in the rearing of their children. The wife is to be in control alone when the husband is incapacitated, absent, etc.

Generally, however, it can be said that the family responsibilities are to be shared as follows:

Husband's Responsibilities. It is normally the husband's obligation to provide for his wife and children. It might be interesting to note that in many foreign societies, the bride's parents still give the groom a *dowry* (the French *dot*). This may be in the form of money, a house, or furniture. Originally, this was done to compensate the groom for taking over the burden of the bride's maintenance from her parents.

Today, its purpose is to make a contribution toward the young couple's initial expense in setting up a household. While this may seem to be an antiquated custom, even the most modern girl has her hope chest and many elaborate wedding gifts are but a dowry by another name.

Wife's Duties. It is normally the wife's responsibility to manage the household, to bear children, and to look after them. Of course, when the wife is the wage-earner instead of the husband, because of his incapacity or otherwise, the roles might be reversed. And, when both the husband and the wife go out to work, a logical compromise in the rearrangement of responsibilities is customary. A husband no longer has the right which he had a scant hundred years ago, of chastising his wife for neglecting her wifely duties.

Consummation. Both parties owe each other a reasonable amount of sexual intercourse. This is considered an integral part of marriage to such an extent that non-consummation can be grounds for an annulment or divorce. (*See* pages 49 and 82.)

Place of Residence. It is technically still the husband's prerogative to decide where to live and according to what standards. The Quebec Civil Code places an express obligation on a wife to live with her husband at the place of his choice, unless the place is dangerous. Conversely, the husband is under an obligation to his wife to let her share his habitation with him. He is not entitled, as of yore, to hold her imprisoned there.

In an English matrimonial case, a woman was held not to have deserted her husband when he retired into monastic seclusion and she refused to follow him into his self-chosen, primitive dwelling. The court decided that the accommodation provided must not be totally unreasonable under the circumstances.

Property Rights. Except in Quebec (discussed separately at the end of this chapter), it is no longer of any special advantage to a Canadian man to marry a rich woman. There may be fringe benefits for him, of course, if she is generous with her wealth; but, if she makes him fulfil the obligations that are imposed on him by law, he may find it quite burdensome to maintain her in the manner to which she is accustomed. Until 1871, a man, upon his marriage, automatically became the owner of practically all that his wife possessed. Today, neither person loses ownership of his belongings to the other.

In Ontario, married women have been entitled to hold separate property since 1884. On the whole, a married woman enjoys just about the same legal status as a man. She may even sit in the English House of Lords today but she cannot become President of the United States of America or drink beer in an Ontario beverage room for men only.

Contracts between Spouses. Except in Quebec, where spouses cannot enter into contracts with one another, husband and wife are free, technically, to sue one another for breach of contract.

Undue Influence. However, if a wife enters into a contract with her husband which turns out to be unfavourable for her, it will be an easy matter for the wife to avoid her liabilities by claiming that she acted under his *undue influence.* The law recognizes the fact that a wife will do anything of a business nature that her husband recommends, out of her love or fear of him. The plea of undue influence is also available to a wife with regard to contracts she has entered into with other people for her husband's benefit; for example, when she guarantees his liabilities. She loses her right to plead undue influence if she has entered into a contract of this nature on the advice of her own, independent lawyer; that is, not a lawyer who also represents her husband's interests.

Torts and Crimes. Generally speaking, there are very few situations surviving today to indicate that, at one time, husband and wife were considered to be one in the eyes of the

law; and that one, usually, being the husband. For example:
• Spouses cannot sue one another in Tort (negligence, trespass, assault, libel, slander, etc.) even if committed before the marriage. And, generally, each spouse is liable to pay damages for any torts against third parties committed by himself; but not for those committed by his spouse. (*See* page 26 for Quebec.)
• One spouse can lay criminal charges against the other, for example, for assault. But a man cannot be guilty of the crime of rape against his wife (unless they are legally separated), and a wife cannot, usually, be guilty of the crime of theft against her husband. There is an exception to this rule when she is on the verge of leaving him or is living separately from him.
• A husband and wife cannot commit the crime of conspiracy with one another, that is, the crime of planning an unlawful act. It takes at least two to conspire. For the purposes of conspiracy, the husband and wife are regarded as one, and "you cannot conspire with yourself."
• A married person cannot be an *accessory after the fact* to a crime committed by his spouse; for example, by hiding or otherwise aiding him, or by helping him to escape. If some other person did this, he would be regarded as a party to the crime, and be punishable along with the principal criminal.
• Subject to certain exceptions listed in the Canada Evidence Act, one spouse cannot be compelled to give evidence against the other in a criminal trial.

Privileged Communications. Communications between husband and wife during *coverture* (while living as husband and wife) are *privileged*. This means that neither spouse can be compelled to tell in the witness box what was said to him by the other. Talking to one's spouse is almost like talking to yourself, and a person certainly cannot be made to testify as to what he said to himself.

Consequently, it is seldom that a breach of confidence is committed when confidential information is revealed to one's spouse; nor is publication of a slander deemed to have taken place by saying something to one's spouse that is defamatory of another person. But a third party is guilty of libel or slander of the one spouse if he makes a defamatory statement about him to the other spouse.

Marriage Brokerage Contracts. Any person who, for a fee, introduces a couple to each other for purposes of matrimony, is disentitled to court assistance if his fee is not paid. Such marriage brokerage contracts are held by Common Law to be illegal, as being against public policy.

While the broker is subject to no punishment, and is not in any way restricted from carrying on his business, he cannot enlist the court's aid if his clients do not pay him. The broker's only safeguard, consequently, is to demand payment in advance.

Creditors' Claims. In view of the fact that a wife today, generally, can have means of her own and the full power to administer them, she alone can be held responsible to honour any contractual obligations she has undertaken. Her husband is **not** automatically responsible to make good his wife's debts and other obligations; nor can the wife's funds be made available to satisfy the claims of her husband's creditors.

Naturally, there are many exceptions to this general rule. One has already been mentioned; namely, when one spouse has, in writing, guaranteed the other spouse's loan or other obligations, after having received independent legal advice.

Bankruptcy Laws. Another exception exists if the debtor spouse has violated any of the Bankruptcy laws which exist for the protection of creditors. For example, he may have been guilty of making an *undue preference*; that is, by paying his wife, in full, a debt that is due to her, before fulfilling his other obligations, with the result that his remaining assets are no longer sufficient to meet, in full, the claims of his other creditors.

Or, a spouse may have effected a *fraudulent conveyance*. For example, a husband may have put money, securities, real estate or personal property, etc., into his wife's name (by gift or for a fictitious purchase price) just before going bankrupt or having his goods and other property seized and sold under a court execution order. Such a transfer can be declared void and the items covered by it will be made available to the debtor-spouse's creditors.

If the transfer was made during the twelve-month period immediately preceding the bankruptcy, it will be presumed to have been fraudulent. If it was made one to five years before the bankruptcy, the transfer will be declared valid if the bankrupt spouse can prove that he was solvent at the time of the transfer, without the items in question.

A wife, of course, may have a perfectly valid claim against

her bankrupt husband but the bankruptcy laws place some claims by a person against his bankrupt spouse in a *deferred category*, as opposed to a secured or preferred or general claim.

If the property was put in the other spouse's name more than five years before the bankruptcy, it is safe from the creditors. The only thing the transferor need then be concerned about is his spouse's trustworthiness. That a woman's faithfulness cannot always be taken for granted is illustrated by the case of a Toronto restaurant owner. Not so many years ago, he sold his well-known establishment with the undertaking that neither he, nor any member of his family, would open and operate a restaurant within a mile of the said business for the next five years. (Such an undertaking is a perfectly binding one. If it had been for a substantially greater length of time and covered a much wider area, it might have been voidable for being in *undue restraint of trade*.)

Reneging on his promise to the purchaser, the previous owner opened a new restaurant a few months later, just around the corner from his old one. To get around his contractual obligation, he put the new restaurant in the name of his mistress. Unfortunately for him, she tired of him, sold the business and made off with the proceeds and her new lover. Legally, her jilted lover was helpless. He could not do a thing.

Agency. Undoubtedly, the most frequent exceptions to the general rule that one spouse is not responsible for the other's contracts are the cases where a wife enters into contract obligations in the capacity of her husband's agent. Agencies can come into existence by various means. For example, a person (the Principal) can make out a formal *Power of Attorney*, giving another person (the Agent) express authority to act for him in certain capacities. The power can range from unlimited authority to dispose over the principal's entire property, to very narrowly delineated powers, for example, to act as the purchasing agent for a small business. Frequently, a person lodges a Power of Attorney with his bank, by which he authorizes his spouse to draw cheques on an account which stands in his name alone.

Another example of an express agency is a *proxy* issued to someone to vote for a shareholder at a company meeting. Yet another common example is the authorization which the owner of a charge account at a store, or an oil company, etc., gives to his spouse and/or his children to charge their purchases to his account.

Implied Agency. An agency can also arise by *implication.* As an example, let us assume that someone (Person A) goes into a store, explaining that he wants to make a purchase which will be paid for by someone else (Person B). Let us further assume that the same store gives the goods to A without checking with B first. Let us also assume that, on the due date, B pays for this purchase without demur or argument. By this series of events, A has, by implication, been appointed B's purchasing agent at that particular store; in fact, at any establishment which has come to learn of B's behaviour on this occasion.

In this example, the store appears to have been unusually trusting. But if they knew B to be a respected member of the community, and A to be his wife, child, or other trusted household member, then their behaviour becomes less surprising.

The consequences of B's course of conduct in voluntarily meeting this obligation are as follows: Should A ever charge something to B's account again, even without B's knowledge or against his wishes, B will have to honour this subsequent obligation.

In addition to these rules, which apply to anybody, a wife is her husband's assumed agent when entering into reasonable contracts for household necessities such as food, supplies, emergency repairs, etc. An Article of the Quebec Civil Code expressly makes the wife an implied agent of her husband's for household purposes.

Termination of Agency. An implied agency continues to exist as long as sensible third parties can conclude reasonably that the agent continues to enjoy the principal's authority. Thus, if a husband-principal wants to put an end effectively to the extravagant shopping sprees of his wife-agent, he must proceed as follows: he must give direct notice (preferably by registered letter) of the termination of his wife's authority to everyone to whom he had honoured her obligations in the past. To protect his credit from being pledged to others in the region who might reasonably regard him as still being prepared to meet her commitments, he should place advertisements in the local press to the effect that he will not pay any debts incurred in his name henceforth by anyone, except with his written authorization. These advertisements are familiar to most people, and they are usually placed by a husband after he and his wife have separated unharmoniously.

Strictly speaking, newspaper advertisements of this nature have legal effect only if the principal can prove that they were read by the creditor. To safeguard himself completely, the principal should advertise in the provincial Gazette. Insertions in this publication constitute *constructive notice* to everyone in the province. The Quebec Civil Code again succinctly states that the wife's implied agency continues until it is expressly and publicly revoked.

Agency by Necessity. A husband can also be made to pay for the purchases of a wife while she was acting as his *agent of necessity*. This can occur when the husband failed in his obligation to provide adequately for her, either while living together or separately. A child, neglected by his parents, can also become an agent of necessity.

Obligations of Parents and Children. All the provinces have legislation regarding the parents' obligation to provide for their children. In Ontario, children are entitled to maintenance and education according to their station in life until they are sixteen or even longer under special circumstances, such as their disability. Violation of this obligation renders the parents liable to three months' imprisonment.

In Quebec, entering into marriage places an obligation on the parents "to maintain their children". In a 1968 case, a well-to-do Montreal father was ordered to pay his forty-four-year-old son $700 a month. The case was appealed with the result yet unknown. Conversely, Quebec children are also under an obligation to maintain their needy parents, grandparents, and those of their spouse. In Ontario, a son or daughter who has the means to do so, can be made to pay up to $20 a week to a parent who is dependent upon him. The Toronto Family Court has about one case a year come up before it involving this provision.

Separate and Joint Property. Let us now recall the statement that the husband and the wife normally continue to own their individual property after marriage in all of Canada except in Quebec. (*See* page 18.) There is no community property in Canada (excluding Quebec) as there is in many of the states in the U.S. In spite of this, it is common for spouses to own property *jointly* (in their joint names).

This means that, after the death of one joint owner, the other becomes the full owner of the jointly owned property, regardless of any provision in the deceased person's will to the contrary. The term *property* technically comprises both land and personal belongings. Houses and bank accounts are the property which is most frequently placed into joint ownership by the spouses. Jointly owned property cannot be sold or otherwise disposed of by one of the owners alone; any contract disposing of it requires the signatures of both. If one cannot sign because of mental illness or because he is an "absentee" the court may order an official representative to sign in his stead. (*See* page 6.)

While the surviving joint owner of property inherits it automatically, the putting of property into joint ownership does not automatically avoid the payment of succession duties, Estate Taxes, or other death duties after the death of one joint owner. If the estate is large enough to warrant it, such duties will have to be paid by the survivor on that share of the value of the property which was contributed by the deceased joint owner.

If the couple have separated and their property has to be divided between them by the court, there are no hard and fast rules for the court to follow. If jointly owned property was acquired, more or less equally, out of the funds of both parties, it will probably be divided equally. However, if the jointly owned property was acquired mainly from the funds of one of the couple, the court will make its disposition on equitable principles. One rule of thumb is that a husband who placed property, which was bought with his funds, in joint ownership, is presumed to have intended to make a gift of a half share in the property to his wife. As a matter of fact, he is excused from the payment of gift tax when making such a once-in-a-lifetime gift to his wife of a half share in a home provided the gift does not exceed $10,000. (*See* page 113.) On the other hand, if the wife pays for jointly-held property from her funds, it is deemed that the entire property is being held in trust for her. If the property is not placed in the joint names of the couple, then the person who paid for the property will be deemed to be its owner. Wedding gifts to the couple do not, necessarily, become their joint property; this might be of particular importance when a substantial present is made by one of the parents. (*See* page 104.)

A partition by the court might also become necessary when a deceased spouse has not made careful disposition of his effects by his will, and there is a dispute among the heirs; or when one of the spouses is declared bankrupt and it has to be determined what part of the family property shall become available to the creditors.

While a wife's earnings belong to her and a husband's earnings belong to him, it has been put forward that a husband's earnings should become joint property. The argument supporting this suggestion is that by her care, devotion, and management, a wife contributes at least as much to the family fortunes as does the husband, the official breadwinner of the family.

It was seen that any gift which a husband makes to his wife becomes her property. But, if he gives her a housekeeping allowance and she does not spend it all, the savings are technically the husband's property.

If one spouse pays for repairs to the other's property, such a payment is generally regarded as a gift to the spouse.

PROVINCIAL VARIATIONS

Quebec

In concluding this chapter, here follow the provisions of the Quebec Civil Code with regard to a married couple's property. The fundamental rule is that a legal *community of property* exists between a husband and wife from the day of their marriage, unless they made previous arrangements to the contrary, or in modification of this rule by a pre-nuptial marriage contract, as will be subsequently explained.

Community Property. Contrary to general belief, not absolutely everything belonging to a husband and wife becomes community property. It includes all the moveable property of both persons, whether it was owned by them before the marriage or was acquired by them during the marriage by purchase, gift, or inheritance, etc. Excepted from the community property are tort damages which are received by one of the spouses for injuries he has suffered, and a wife's earnings from her independent work. As a point of interest, if a married woman, not only in Quebec, has been slandered by an unfounded impugning of her chastity, she is entitled to damages without having to prove any specific financial loss.

Immovables. Not included in the community property is immovable property, such as land, houses, etc., which was owned by the persons previous to the marriage or which they inherit during the marriage. However, immovables which have been acquired by purchase, lease, etc., during the marriage, are included in the community property. By the pre-nuptial contract, the couple legally can agree to include all their immovables, to limit the community property, or to own the community property in unequal shares.

Administration. The right to administer the community property belongs to the husband alone. However, he still requires his wife's agreement for the sale or mortgaging of the immovables or for any gifts of substantial portions of the community property to third parties. The wife's consent is not required when he wants to dispose of property which is his alone.

The wife has the right to administer that part of the property which is hers alone, as distinct from community property. But, with regard to her immovable property, she still cannot sell or mortgage it, or grant a longer lease on it than nine years, without her husband's consent.

Any revenue produced by the wife's privately owned property becomes community property. Any damages or fines which either person has been ordered to pay by the courts, are payable out of the community property.

The husband can obtain an order allowing him to administer his wife's own property if the court feels that she is mismanaging her property, or if she does not turn the revenue from her private property over to the community property.

Dissolution of the Community Property. After the solemnization of the marriage, the parties to it cannot, voluntarily, dissolve or separate the community property. It can be dissolved into equal shares only by the death of one of the couple, a judicial separation, or an annulment of the marriage. Since Quebec had no divorce procedure until recently, divorce is not mentioned in the Civil Code at all. The Code also provides for a division of the property if one of the persons disappears more or less permanently, or if the court grants a wife's application to that effect on one of the following grounds:

- That her interests are imperilled.
- That her husband's affairs are in a disordered state.
- That her husband has abandoned her and she is forced to make her own living.

- For any other serious reason, making it necessary to safeguard her interests.

There are innumerable Articles in the Civil Code, making very involved and detailed provisions for determining what items form part of the community property when it is separated, with particular regard for the rights and interests of the creditors and the heirs on both sides.

The Pre-Nuptial Marriage Contract. If the parties to the contemplated marriage do not like the institution of community property, they can exclude it completely or modify it, by a *pre-nuptial marriage contract.* This contract must be drawn up in *notarial form,* and most certainly before, and not after, the marriage ceremony. As mentioned earlier, no change of a financial nature can be made after the marriage, except that the husband may take out insurance on his life for the benefit of his family.

A marriage contract can also be entered into by a minor, with the assistance of his *tutor.* By his marriage, the minor becomes *emancipated,* but a *curator* is appointed to assist him with his contracts and his law suits. (*See* page 14.)

If the marriage contract excluded community property completely, a wife retains the full rights of administration and the unrestricted right of disposition over her property.

Dower Rights. To compensate a Quebec wife partially for her secondary role, financially speaking, during her husband's lifetime, she gets substantial *dower rights* over her husband's immovable property after his death. This means that she obtains the right to receive, for the rest of her life, one half of the income which his immovable property produces or which it could produce if it were worked or rented out. The right of dower grants the dead man's children the legal title to the full ownership of one half of his immovable property.

The wife also obtains these dower rights after a judicial separation from her husband which was due to his fault. The husband cannot deprive his wife of the dower rights by his will. She forfeits these rights only if the court finds her guilty of adultery, desertion, or if she has voluntarily signed away her dower rights, partially or completely, in the pre-nuptial marriage contract. If a man marries a second time, the second wife's dower rights are subject to the dower rights of the children of the first marriage.

Ontario

Dower Rights. In Ontario, a widow, on the death of her husband, "may tarry in his chief house for forty days after his death"; this is her right of *quarantine*. She also has dower rights for her lifetime to one third of the income from her deceased husband's fully owned, improved, private real estate. In other words, she receives income from the non-mortgaged portion of the house and grounds used for the deceased husband's home, not bought purely for business or investment. Therefore, when a person buys land in Ontario, or lends money to its owner under a mortgage, he must be sure to get the signature not only of the man who owns the land outright but also the signature of the owner's wife. By signing the deed, she "bars her inchoate right of dower" even if she is under twenty-one years of age. If this is omitted, the buyer of a $30,000 home, for example, runs the risk of having to pay the the interest on $10,000 to the widow of the seller for the rest of her life.

Where a wife is shown to be of unsound mind, or is on bad terms with and separated from her husband, a judge may grant an order making her signature unnecessary.

If the buyer's lawyer, when "searching the title", failed to notice the absence of such a signature, he would be financially responsible to his client to make up such a loss caused by his professional negligence. Lawyers and other professional people habitually carry *malpractice insurance* against contingencies of this nature.

Dower rights cannot be taken away arbitrarily from his wife by the husband's will. What often happens, however, is that the will offers her more favourable terms if she voluntarily renounces her dower rights. As has just been illustrated, she has the power to do this effectively by her signature to the deed. (*See* pages 105 and 107.)

Estate by the Curtesy. In Ontario, there still exists a widower's right, *by the Curtesy of England*, to a life interest in all of his deceased wife's real estate, provided she bore him a live child at some time during their marriage. This right is easily extinguishable by the wife, however, by the mere act of selling, or deeding, the land over her own signature; or, by making a will, in which she leaves the land to someone else.

Other Provinces

In the Western provinces (from Manitoba to British Columbia) there exist *homestead rights,* which virtually amount to joint ownership of the family home. To obtain such rights in British Columbia, a wife must first register her claim to them. In Newfoundland, dower and curtesy rights have been abolished, as they also have been in England and in many of the states in the U.S.

chapter 4

LEGAL SEPARATION

When a marriage goes sour there is nothing, in theory, to prevent a couple from agreeing to go their own separate ways. In reality, however, it is seldom that easy. Even after a short marriage, too many elements of the couple, both tangible and intangible, have become intermingled. If there are any children involved, a separation of the parents becomes a very grave matter, indeed.

There are three basic ways to end a marriage: legal separation, annulment, and divorce. This chapter deals with legal separation alone. Annulment and divorce are discussed in the following chapters.

JUDICIAL SEPARATION

Most of the provinces in Canada have machinery for obtaining a judicial separation and for enforcing the terms accompanying the separation order. Such a judicial separation can also be called a "divorce from bed and board". This is quite distinct from a "divorce from the marriage shackles", the full term for what is more commonly known merely as a *divorce*.

An official separation order releases the couple from the obligation of living together, but it does not entitle them to marry anyone else during the other's lifetime. After a judicial separation or after entering into a separation agreement, neither person can technically be found guilty of deserting the other. The husband can no longer be held legally responsible for the payment of purchases of necessities made by his estranged wife, provided he continues maintaining her financially, according to the terms of the separation order or agreement. (*See* Appendix.)

WHY JUDICIAL SEPARATION?

A judicial separation may be granted by the court at the request of one marriage partner, even against the wishes of the other, provided there exist certain grounds for the granting of a separation order. Instead of a divorce, a separation might be requested for any of the following reasons:

- The petitioner does not believe in divorce, on religious or other grounds.
- It is not possible, or too difficult, or too expensive to get a divorce.
- The petitioner cannot satisfy the necessary domicile requirements for a divorce. (*See* page 52.)
- The petitioner does not have sufficient grounds for a divorce.
- It might be to the petitioner's financial advantage to remain married to a spouse who is likely to predecease him.
- The required length of time, which would entitle him to a divorce, has not yet elapsed.
- The petitioner hopes for a possible reconciliation.

PROVINCIAL LAWS

Here follow the laws concerning judicial separation, province by province. Perhaps, federal legislation will be passed some day, making the laws regarding separations and annulments uniform throughout Canada.

Ontario and Prince Edward Island are discussed first by virtue of their lack of judicial separation laws. Quebec follows because it is the third of the provinces in which the separation laws differ radically from those of the seven remaining provinces. The law of judicial separation in these provinces follows the law of England, as it existed at various times before 1870.

Ontario

By a quirk of law-making, the Ontario courts no longer have the power to order judicial separations of marriages. The 1930 federal Act, which granted Ontario the power to decree the dissolution and annulment of marriages, inadvertently took away all other rights which Ontario previously had regarding matrimonial causes.

As a result, marriage separations in Ontario are not granted by the courts, but can come about purely by a mutual agreement by the couple. To safeguard the interests of both, a carefully worded separation agreement should be drawn up and signed by them, preferably after consultation with their lawyers. A sample agreement will be found in the Appendix, on page 115. A violation of the agreement would constitute a breach of contract, for which a remedy can be sought in the courts. And, if a separated husband neglects to provide for his family adequately, the Family Court will, independently of any contract, compel him to fulfil his financial obligations as a husband which, at law, he continues to be. Failure to maintain his family by a man who has the financial means to do so, may result in his imprisonment. (*See* page 40.)

Invalid Separation Agreements. Separation agreements are of legal value only if they are drawn up after the couple have decided to separate from one another. A separation agreement which provides for some future separation is void. The reason for this is that such an agreement might constitute an inducement to separate and is, thus, contrary to public policy. It makes no difference whether the premature separation agreement was drawn up before, or during, the marriage.

On the other hand, an agreement making advance provision for what is to happen in case the couple is divorced, is valid. Also valid is a separation agreement made in advance by a couple living apart, but planning a reconciliation. Such an agreement is not held to be against public policy, since its basic objective is to facilitate something desirable, namely a reconciliation.

Another point worth emphasizing is that, while a separation releases a couple from the obligation to live together, it does not entitle them to remarry, or to have sexual intercourse with anyone else, even if the agreement is worded so as to permit it. Such conduct amounts to adultery with its subsequent legal consequences.

Naturally, a separation agreement is also void if it was entered into fraudulently, under duress, or otherwise without genuine consent. A separation, whether judicial or by agreement, is ended when the couple resumes cohabitation permanently.

Prince Edward Island

This province is the only one, besides Ontario, in which

judicial separations are not obtainable. While there is nothing, constitutionally, to prevent the Prince Edward Island courts from allowing judicial separation, there appear to be no grounds of any nature specified anywhere in the province for the granting of such separations. Consequently, separation procedure in Prince Edward Island is, substantially, the same as in Ontario.

Quebec

Judicial separation is a particularly common way for unsuccessful Quebec marriages to end, because the Quebec courts did not grant full divorces before September, 1968, and divorce is against the religious beliefs of the predominantly Roman Catholic population of the province.

The Quebec courts will not enforce a separation agreement which has been entered into voluntarily by the separated couple, even if it was formally drawn up in writing. But, the courts will order a judicial separation, whose terms it will then enforce to the utmost, on the following grounds laid down by the Quebec Civil Code:

- Adultery by either spouse. Until recently, a wife could obtain a separation order on the basis of her husband's adultery, only "if he committed the adultery complained of, with his concubine in the marital habitation". This proviso is no longer in effect.
- "Outrage, ill-usage, or grievous insult" committed by either of the spouses.
- A husband's failure to receive his wife into his home.
- A husband's failure to furnish his wife with the necessities of life, according to his circumstances.

Pending the outcome of the separation hearing, the husband has the provisional care of the children, and the wife is entitled to an *alimentary pension* (alimony) and her clothing.

After the separation order, the couple need no longer live together. The family property is separated as follows:

- The wife is allotted whatever is regarded as her separate property.
- The husband must return to his wife any dowry that she brought into the marriage.
- The community property is partitioned. (*See* page 26.)

Alberta and Saskatchewan

These two provinces have incorporated the English law in

provincial statutes of their own, which are almost identical in wording and in substance.

The provincial Superior Courts have jurisdiction with regard to judicial separation and related matters, over parties who are domiciled or resident in the province at the time of the commencement of the action, or who had a matrimonial home in the province when their cohabitation ceased, or the events occurred on which the claim for separation is based.

A judicial separation will be ordered by the court if it finds that either the husband or the wife has, since the solemnization of the marriage, been guilty of:

- Cruelty, (*See* page 77.)
- Unjustified *desertion* for at least two years, (*See* page 35.)
- Failure to comply with a judgment for *restitution of conjugal rights,* (*See* page 39.)
- Sodomy or bestiality, actual or attempted, (*See* page 67.)
- Adultery (*see* page 57), which has not been *connived* at (*see* page 65) by the plaintiff.

A petition for a separation based on adultery *may* be rejected if the plaintiff has been guilty of conduct *conducing* to the adultery. (*See* page 90.)

In addition to the last two *bars to relief,* that is connivance and conducing conduct, a separation will not be granted if:

- The plaintiff has *condoned,* forgiven, any of the previously mentioned matrimonial offences. (*See* page 66.)
- The plaintiff and the respondent have been guilty of *collusion* in presenting the claim. (*See* page 64.)
- The plaintiff has committed adultery which has not been condoned by the respondent.

British Columbia, Manitoba, New Brunswick, Newfoundland, Nova Scotia and The Territories

In these provinces, the pre-1857 laws of judicial separation, as originally exercised in the old Ecclesiastical Courts of England, are perpetuated. The grounds for a judicial separation were, and are:

- Adultery
- Cruelty
- Unwarranted desertion for at least two years
- Unsoundness of mind
- Rape, committed by a husband, and his actual or attempted sodomy or bestiality.

The separation order may be withheld if any of the previously-mentioned bars to relief exist.

For a person to institute proceedings for judicial separation, he must be a resident of the province from whose courts he seeks the desired relief. He need not, necessarily, have his legal domicile there. (*See* page 52.)

DESERTION

Definition. Possibly, the most common of all matrimonial offences is the desertion of one spouse by the other. There is no statutory definition for desertion, but fundamentally it consists of the wilful cessation of cohabitation by the one party, without just cause, and without the consent of the other.

Since cohabitation consists of living together in the same place, while rendering one another both sexual and social companionship, and each one performing the household responsibilities normally expected of him, desertion is not deemed to have taken place, unless all these features have terminated. To constitute desertion, in other words, a physical separation between both persons must have taken place, coupled with one person's intention not to return to the other. One of these elements alone, does not suffice.

The simplest example of desertion consists of the irresponsible husband, or flighty wife, packing up and leaving for good. However, *constructive desertion* can also take place when one person, by his conduct, virtually forces the other to leave the matrimonial home, or otherwise to cease full cohabitation. Under such circumstances, it is not the person who left the premises who is guilty of desertion, but the one who drove him to it. There are numerous examples to illustrate these rules.

Insufficient Physical Separation. In the following decided cases, it was held that there was **not** sufficient physical separation to constitute desertion:

- The husband and wife slept in different rooms and kept conversation to an unavoidable minimum; the wife continuing to cook the husband's meals, however.
- The couple slept in different bedrooms, the one spouse refusing sexual intercourse to the other consistently, but otherwise keeping house together.
- The wife refused sexual intercourse and refused to perform any wifely duties at all. In fact, she spent all her

available time with another man, but continued living in the same room with her husband, during emergency war-time conditions.

- The estranged spouses continued occupying a three-room flat.

The last two cases seem to indicate that close physical contiguity will defeat any attempt to establish a separation.

Constructive Physical Separation. The following cases illustrate that physical separation **can** be held to exist, even if the couple continue to live under the same roof provided that, in effect, they are living in two different homes under that roof.

- The husband moved into the basement with his mother, who looked after his underground household for him completely.
- The couple lived completely separate lives in a five-room bungalow, except for sharing the kitchen, which they used at different times whenever possible.
- The husband padlocked his bedroom and ate all of his meals outside the house.

Matrimonial Home. The husband is also, technically, guilty of desertion, if he fails in his duty to provide a matrimonial home, which is reasonably adequate, according to his circumstances. As we have already seen, a monk's cell could not be so labelled. (*See* page 17.)

An interesting extension to this rule was demonstrated in a case where a husband, before the marriage, agreed to make his wife's place of business their matrimonial home. After the marriage, the husband moved to another house, without any change in the couple's circumstances having taken place, and demanded that his wife join him there. When his wife refused to accompany him, it was he who was held to be constructively guilty of desertion.

Intention to Desert. In addition to being physically absent, the second vital element of desertion is the intention not to return. This intention is assumed to exist in an absent spouse, unless he can give a satisfactory explanation for his absence.

Excused Absences. The following are grounds for being absent without committing desertion:

- Absence on business. In one case, a businessman was held

justified in refusing to take his wife along with him to India, because of her extravagant habits.

- To seek employment.
- For the good of one's health.
- The absent spouse's insanity at the time of his leaving.
- Imprisonment, or attempts to evade it. However, failure to return home after having been released from prison, was held to amount to desertion. Similarly guilty of desertion was the man who, while eluding the clutches of the law, did so in the company of a lady friend, without informing his wife to that effect at the time.

Consent. To constitute desertion, as previously stated, the one person's departure or absence must have taken place without the other's consent, either expressed or implied. It follows that, in order to succeed in his claim on the basis of desertion, the deserted person must, at all times, be willing to take back the deserter. By refusing to take back a deserter who has made a genuine offer to return, the deserted spouse is consenting to the separation by implication, with the result that the absence no longer constitutes desertion.

A deserter is not purged of his offence by making regular payments to his deserted wife; nor is she deemed to consent to his absence by accepting these payments. The two-year period of absence is not interrupted if the couple meet occasionally to attempt a reconciliation, not even if the meetings are accompanied by sexual intercourse.

Apart from an express refusal to receive the absent person back, such an intention was attributed to a wife who changed all the locks of the house after her husband's departure.

Examples of offers to return which were held not to be genuine were an offer by a deserter to return without resuming sexual intercourse, and a husband's offer to return to his wife with the proviso that he be allowed to continue his affair with another woman.

We have seen that a separation agreement drawn up between the couple precludes the possibility of desertion. (*See* page 30.) This is the case not only when the agreement was drawn up before the separation, but also if it was entered into after the departure of the one spouse.

Constructive Desertion. The following are examples of *constructive desertion*, that is behaviour by the one spouse which was considered sufficiently aggravating to drive the other away from home with good cause. As a consequence, desertion was committed not by the person departing, but by the person causing the other to leave.

- The stay-at-home has literally thrown the other out of the house, or ordered him out. For this expulsion to count as constructive desertion, it must have been committed deliberately, and not in the heat of a bitter argument resulting in frayed tempers.
- One spouse has committed adultery, or cruelty.
- One spouse has inflicted physical violence on the other, or been guilty of other "grave and weighty conduct", falling short of actual cruelty.
- A husband's sexual malpractices on his wife.
- Excessive or revolting sexual demands.
- Grave sexual misconduct with third parties.
- Incest with his child.
- Wilful and unjustifiable refusal of sexual intercourse. **Note:** a wife's fear of conception does not justify her refusal.
- Intolerable excesses of temper, not just a poor disposition.
- Heavy drinking, resulting in violence, or in delirium tremens.
- Treason by an army officer's wife, resulting in her conviction.
- Giving the other person reason to believe that he is carrying on an adulterous association.
- A husband's failure to provide an adequate home.

Unpenalized Conduct. The following cases illustrate conduct which was not held to be constructive desertion:

- Selfishness, lack of consideration, or a sour disposition, resulting in the other's unhappiness.
- A wife's laziness and dirtiness either personal or in her housekeeping.
- A farmer preferring the company of his pigman (with no suggestion of homosexuality) to that of his wife, to the extent of neglecting her almost completely.
- Refusal of intercourse through invincible repugnance to the sexual act, or through structural incapacity caused by an accident or disease, subsequent to the marriage.
- A wife's admission that she loves another man.
- A neurotic condition, unaccompanied by other aggravating features.

- Venereal disease, innocently contracted before the marriage.
- The wife tricking her husband into marriage, claiming to be pregnant by him.
- Premarital pregnancy by another man.
- A conviction for a criminal offence, short of constituting cruelty.

Restitution of Conjugal Rights. In those provinces where desertion constitutes grounds for a judicial separation, it must have lasted for two years. This period can be shortened, however, if the following procedure is adopted:

1. The deserted person makes a written demand for a resumption of cohabitation to the other person. Making this request is a step which can be omitted, if the circumstances of the case show that such a demand is obviously useless, for example, if the deserter has lodged a petition for divorce.
2. If the deserter has not responded to this demand favourably, the deserted person seeks from the court a judgment, ordering a *Restitution of Conjugal Rights.* This order will not be granted against someone who is away just for a holiday, etc.
3. The deserter's non-compliance with this order is tantamount to two years' desertion, for judicial separation purposes.

If the deserter complies with the order by returning, he cannot be compelled to resume sexual intercourse.

Jactitation of Marriage. This seems to be the most appropriate point to mention a remedy which exists in seven provinces, to silence a person "A" who, without the other person's "B's", consent or acquiescence, persistently and falsely alleges or boasts that he is married to the other person, "B". By bringing an action for *Jactitation of Marriage,* "B" may obtain a judgment ordering "A", the maker of the allegations, to be perpetually silent on the subject.

In provinces such as Ontario, where no such action lies, the court could be asked to issue an injunction, restraining any repetition of the false claims.

Alimony, Maintenance, Custody of Children. The financial arrangements and other matters associated with, and consequent upon separation proceedings, are dealt with in chapter 9. However, provision is made in all the provinces for families which have been deserted by the husband. Provincial statutes enable proceedings to be taken against the husband for financial support without, necessarily, requesting a separation order.

The following is a summary of the Ontario statute. Its provisions are basically the same in the other provinces.

Deserted Wives and Children's Maintenance Act. No great detail of the Act is given here because deserted wives are not uncommon, unfortunately, and the information clerk at the nearest Family Court can tell her exactly how she should proceed to attain her rights. There is no similar provision for a husband with a large family of small children whose wife has walked out on her obligations, or for a sick husband whose wife beats him up periodically.

If a husband has deserted his family without providing maintenance for his wife and children, he can be summoned before the court, even if the couple has separated formally. The summons can be issued by a Justice of the Peace after an interview with the deserted wife, or with the person who has the custody of a motherless child. At a hearing before one of the Family Courts, which are established throughout Ontario, the judge or the Magistrate may order the husband to make whatever payments seem fair under the circumstances, provided he has the means to pay. If the hearing takes place in a province where there are no Family Courts, the Magistrate's Court will conduct the hearing. The maximum amount payable with regard to each deserted child is $20 a week.

Desertion is also held to have taken place if the wife is living apart from her husband because the husband:

- Fails to supply his wife and children with food and the necessities of life,
- Is guilty of cruelty,
- Or, has committed adultery which the wife has not condoned. (*See* page 66.)

If the husband does not keep up the payments which he has been ordered to make, he can be summoned before the court. If he fails to obey the summons, he can be arrested. And, if he is found to have the means to pay, he can be imprisoned for a term not exceeding three months, or until he pays the required amount, whichever occurs first.

A Justice of the Peace has the power to order the arrest of

a man who is about to leave the Justice's jurisdiction in order to avoid appearing at his court.

If the deserted wife is, or is about to become, a public charge upon the community, the delinquent husband can be ordered to report regularly to a probation officer. Failure to comply with this order is punishable by imprisonment up to three months.

A wife who has been granted a maintenance order against her husband, loses the relief granted to her if she commits adultery which is not condoned by her husband.

The wife of a lunatic or a convict, or a deserted woman who is entitled to a maintenance order, can get a court order entitling her to the earnings of her minor children.

chapter 5

ANNULMENT

The law concerning the annulment of marriages has not been changed by the Divorce Act of 1968. As a result, each province continues to be governed by the same laws as before the passage of the Act. The courts of all the provinces and Territories hear annulment petitions; even Quebec and Newfoundland, where no divorce actions could be tried before 1968. As yet there appear to have been no annulment actions in Prince Edward Island. There are only insignificant variations in the law between the provinces, because the laws with regard to annulment are based on the Common Law, which in turn, inherited them from the Ecclesiastical Law.

The Ontario courts were faced with a problem when the new Divorce Act was passed. While the Act does not deal with annulments, it repealed the 1930 federal Act which granted the Ontario courts jurisdiction in dissolutions and annulments of marriage. Therefore, it appeared temporarily that there were to be no more annulments in Ontario. However, a 1933 amendment to the Ontario Marriage Act had made the 1930 federal Act a part of Ontario law, so that the Ontario courts have not lost jurisdiction in nullity proceedings after all.

An annulment order does not dissolve an existing marriage. Instead, it is an official court declaration to the effect that a particular union does not constitute a legal marriage. In fact, in most cases, the order declares that the marriage was void *ab initio*, that it never did exist. As a result, the engagement ring should be returned after an annulment while after a divorce or separation, a wife is entitled to keep it. It will be remembered that an engagement ring is an example of a gift with a condition attached to it, in this case, that a marriage will take place.

GROUNDS FOR ANNULMENT

An annulment will be ordered on the following grounds (all, except the last, will declare the marriage to have been void *ab initio*):

- One of the parties to the marriage lacked the legal capacity to contract a marriage because of:
  - A prior marriage,
  - Tender years,
  - Mental incompetence, or
  - Consanguinity or affinity to the other party.
- One of the parties did not genuinely consent to becoming married due to:
  - Fear or duress, or
  - Fundamental mistake or error.
- There was a grave defect in the formalities associated with the marriage.
- One or both of the parties is impotent.

As mentioned before, a marriage which is annulled on the grounds of impotence is not automatically void *ab initio*. The marriage is said to be voidable, and it becomes void as of the moment when the decree of nullity is pronounced.

HISTORY

While there are still plenty of annulment cases, their number is relatively insignificant when compared to the number of annulments which were ordered before divorces became possible. Annulments still play an important part for unhappily married Catholics, of course, who do not believe in divorce.

While the Pope has always possessed the power to dissolve a marriage, he has rarely exercised it. Consequently, the authorities often went to extremes to grant nullity declarations. The rules of prohibited consanguinity and affinity were often stretched. For example, a marriage was annulled because the two parties to it were related in the seventh degree, and by marriage at that. In another case, a man's marriage was declared void because he had pre-marital sexual intercourse with a third cousin of his future wife.

Another ground for annulment was the existence of a *precontract*, whereby one of the parties had, before the marriage, made a binding promise to marry someone else. Today this is no longer grounds for an annulment, but as we have already seen, it might entitle the victim of the breach of the precontract to compensation.

MARRIAGES VOID *Ab Initio*

In bigamy, as well as in all the other cases of void "marriages" which follow, it is not necessary, strictly speaking, to obtain a decree of nullity from the court. If a person is completely sure that his "marriage" is void, he can take a chance and get married to someone else. If it turns out that he has appraised his status correctly, he will have behaved quite properly and be subject to no penalty. It is far wiser, however, to have one's status clarified by obtaining a decree of annulment which, as was stated earlier, officially declares a "marriage" to be void. Such a decree is also a *sine qua non* with regard to the partitioning of the family property, the clearing of the title to real property, and to a clarification of the situation with regard to the claims of creditors and potential heirs.

On the other hand, if a couple want to stay together, and fear that their marriage is void for one reason or another, they would be wise to marry one another again once the impediment to their marriage has been removed. For example, they may legally marry when an earlier spouse (the cause of the bigamous marriage) has died or secured a divorce.

In the case of those "marriages" which are void *ab initio*, a decree of nullity can be requested not only by the two most concerned parties, but by any interested party. It can be sought not only during the lifetime of the two principal parties (it would be technically incorrect to call them spouses) but even after the death of one of them.

In Ontario, any children which are born of a union which is subsequently declared void, are considered legitimate, provided their parents formed the union in good faith, without being aware of any irregularity. (*See* page 6.)

LACK OF LEGAL CAPACITY

Bigamy. The term bigamy is used loosely here; bigamy is a crime which is committed when a person goes through a marriage ceremony when he knows, or ought to know, that he is still married. However, whether he knows or not, any union he forms while still married to another, is not a valid marriage, but is completely void. Theoretically, the victim of bigamy can sue the bigamist for damages for the tort of deceit or for breach of the implied warranty he gave that he was free to marry.

A person who has successfully petitioned for divorce (or for annulment on the grounds of impotence) receives a provisional *decree nisi*[1] first which is usually made into a final *decree absolute* three months later. (*See* page 95.) Such a person is not free to marry again until he has received the *decree absolute,* and any marriage which he attempts to enter earlier is void.

Also void is any marriage which has been entered into during a compulsory waiting period which had been imposed by the court. For example, the court might have ordered that neither person could marry until the expiry of the time allowed for a possible appeal from the divorce decree. Our courts have ignored, however, a purely punitive waiting period which had been imposed by a foreign court. In that case, the guilty party in the divorce proceedings was prohibited by the court from remarrying until the blameless party had married again.

A previous marriage in a Hindu ceremony incapacitates a person from marrying again, even though the Hindu marriage is potentially bigamous.

A marriage is void after the return-to-life of a previous spouse who had been legally presumed dead. (*See* page 6.) This dilemma can now be avoided because a long-absent spouse can be divorced under the new Divorce Act. (*See* page 81.) It is interesting to note that annulment proceedings can be initiated not only by an innocent victim of bigamy, but also by the bigamist.

Lack of Age. Previously we have discussed, province by province, the age under which it is illegal to get married, and under which parental consent to a marriage is required. (See chapter 3.) It should be remembered that the lack of parental consent does not, usually, invalidate a marriage. However, lack of the minimum age requirements is grounds for invalidating a marriage subject to the exceptions specified in the different provinces: in some it is the young wife's pregnancy; in others it is sexual intercourse by the couple after the

1 *Nisi* is Latin for "if not" or "unless." This indicates that the decree will be made final in due course, unless valid reasons are adduced in the meantime why this should not be done.

marriage, and sometimes, even before the marriage. In England, a marriage by anyone under sixteen years of age, is void without exception.

In Quebec, an annulment can be initiated by a person whose consent to the marriage should have been obtained, but who failed to give it. Anybody can attack the validity of a Quebec marriage on the grounds of lack of age, but he must do so within six months of the marriage, provided the wife is not pregnant. A young person's *family council* can attack the validity of a marriage, if his curator gave his consent to the marriage, without first fulfilling his obligation to consult the family council. The family council has similar rights in connection with a marriage to an insane person. (*See* page 5.)

Mental Incompetence. For an annulment petition which is based on mental incompetence to succeed, it must be shown that the person whose insanity is being pleaded was quite unaware of the significance of the marriage ceremony. He must have been in a state of imbecility or idiocy, at the time. A moronic intelligence does not disqualify a person from marriage. In one instance, the application to have a marriage to a schizophrenic annulled was refused because the schizophrenia did not develop until soon after the marriage. The fact that, at the time of the marriage, he was mentally ill to a lesser degree, did not suffice to warrant an annulment.

A marriage during a lucid interval of a mentally ill person is valid, unless he has been certified insane.

For a marriage to be annulled because of drunkenness, the drunkenness at the time of the marriage must amount to the degree described just previously.

Consanguinity or Affinity. The relationships existing between a couple which are either of a permitted or prohibited degree for marriage between them have already been mentioned. (*See* page 5.) Throughout Canada, marriage is permitted between first cousins, but not between anyone more closely related. In some of the states in the U.S. even fifth cousins are regarded as being too closely related for marriage to be permitted between them, the so-called "kissing cousins." All the provinces, including British Columbia, now permit a marriage between a man and his living divorced wife's sister, and between a man and his living brother's divorced wife.

If a prohibited degree of relationship is found to exist between two people, their "marriage" is void. As is generally known, sexual intercourse between brothers and sisters, parents and children, grandparents and grandchildren, uncles and nieces, etc., is the crime of incest if the parties were aware of the relationship, and is severely punishable.

LACK OF CONSENT

Fear and Duress. If a person marries to prevent death or serious injury to himself, he has grounds for petitioning that his marriage be annulled. Consequently, the notorious "shotgun weddings" (in which the girl's father pointed a gun at the head of the groom) are subject to annulment. There were cases in 1894 and in 1938 where women had their marriages annulled because they married men who had previously threatened to kill them if they did not marry them.

Another illustration of a marriage entered into through fear is the case of a girl in an Iron Curtain country. Soon after World War II, she married an obliging foreign friend purely as a means to escape the country in which she feared for her life and safety. There was no consummation of the marriage and she obtained an annulment. But the Englishman who thought that he would be allowed to bring his Russian wife to England with him, was not granted an annulment when he found she was not allowed to leave her country. Apparently, there was no fear or duress involved in her case, and the man's mistaken belief that she would be permitted to leave the USSR was not sufficient grounds for an annulment. This marriage, incidentally, was consummated.

A recent illustration of fear constituting lack of consent occurred in 1967 when a man living in Malta, was arrested and falsely charged with corrupting a young girl. Upon the advice of his lawyer and his employer, he married the girl rather than face a prison term. When he returned to England, he was granted an annulment because he acted from substantial fear, with good cause, and because the fear arose from circumstances for which he was not to blame.

Error or Mistake. To constitute grounds for annulment, the mistake must be of a fundamental nature, such as a mistake regarding the nature of the ceremony, or the identity of the person one is marrying. Other mistakes, even such an important one as was seen in the case of the Russian wife, are insufficient. Nor does it constitute sufficient grounds for an annulment if the one person was mistaken about the other's wealth, social standing, name, title, criminal record, chastity, pregnancy, or the existence of a child or children (ten in a recent U.S. case!), even if the mistake was caused by the other person's fraud. If the fraud is discovered before the wedding, it would entitle the victim to break off the engagement and to sue for any damages suffered as a consequence. (*See* page 3.)

Concerning mistakes about the other person, only a mistake regarding his identity would invalidate the marriage. In the absence of an actual case, an imaginary illustration would be a deaf and blind person accidentally getting married to the wrong person in a multiple marriage ceremony.

The following cases illustrate mistakes as to the nature of the marriage ceremony which were sufficient to invalidate the marriage:

- A woman mistakenly married a Hindu, in the belief that the ceremony was a conversion ceremony to the Hindu religion.
- A recent immigrant to Ontario who did not understand English went through a civil marriage ceremony in the belief that it was a betrothal ceremony, which is customary in her country. This mistake is not likely to happen in those provinces which require the ceremony to be translated into the language of the participants. (*See* page 14.) In this case, as in the preceding one, non-consummation of the marriage was considered strong evidence that the alleged lack of consent was completely genuine.

As long as a genuine mistake existed, it does not matter if it was caused by fraud or by a misunderstanding. However, the court will be suspicious of an action based on lack of consent, if it is not lodged within a reasonably short time after discovering the mistake; or after the source of fear, which caused the marriage, ceased to exist. In Quebec, there is a specific time limit of six months for initiating an annulment, and proceedings based on lack of consent can be initiated only by the victim. Mistake, incidentally, is one of the most frequent grounds on which annulment actions are based in Quebec followed by actions based on errors in form, discussed next.

FORMAL DEFECT

An error or irregularity in the form of the marriage ceremony seldom serves as a basis for annulment, except perhaps in Quebec. There may be penalties imposed on the couple, or on a licencing or marriage official who violated the required formalities, but the marriage will usually stand, particularly if the wife is pregnant or if the couple has had sexual intercourse with one another. Only a few exceptions come to mind:

- Wong v. Wong. The marriage of a woman was annulled by an Ontario court because she had resided in Ontario for only a week before the marriage instead of for the prescribed fifteen days. The reason for annulling the marriage for such a relatively insignificant technicality was, that the woman had received permission to enter Canada from Hong Kong only upon her assuring the Department of Immigration that her purpose in coming to Canada was to marry a man who had already taken up residence here. Actually, this was only a ruse to gain entry to Canada; the couple at no time cohabited, and the marriage was, obviously, one in name only.
- An English marriage is void if both parties to it deliberately gave false particulars when applying for the marriage banns.
- Lack of the required medical certificate in Alberta, renders the marriage void. (*See* page 10.) It is possible, of course, for the parties to remarry one another immediately afterwards, provided they obtain the necessary certificate, or remedy whatever other defect may have existed temporarily.
- In Manitoba, an annulment on the grounds of formal defect can be sought only within one year of the marriage.
- In Quebec, formal defect is of greater significance than in the other provinces because divorce is not available to true Catholics. Therefore, it is natural to take full advantage of any available legal technicalities to relieve unhappy situations.

IMPOTENCE

(In Prince Edward Island, the term *frigidity* is used.) This is the only ground for annulment which does not render a marriage void *ab initio*. If impotence is not pleaded by the husband or the wife, the marriage stands, even if there exists a clearly established case of impotence. In other words, impotence renders a marriage voidable at the option of one, or both of the parties. It is not automatically rendered void from the beginning, but the annulment declares void a marriage which has legally existed, until then.

In this type of annulment action, a woman will use her married name instead of her maiden name which she uses in the other types of annulment actions. Thus, an action begun by a woman on the basis of her husband's (Mr. Smith's) alleged impotence will be entitled "Smith (otherwise Jones) v. (*versus,* or *against*) Smith" whereas if she applied for an annulment on any other grounds, the action would be entitled "Jones (*falsely called,* or *otherwise,* or *orse.* Smith) v. Smith."

In impotence cases, one marriage partner usually puts forward the other's impotence as the grounds for annulment, but a person can also plead his own impotence in *bona fide* cases, particularly if he was ignorant of his impotence previous to the marriage. An example of proceedings which were held not to be brought bona fide (on sincere grounds), was a case brought on the basis of the other party's impotence, eight years after finding out about his condition. At the other end of the time scale, seven days was held to be sufficient time for experienced marriage partners to find out about a case of impotence.

Nobody but the marriage partners can initiate annulment proceedings on the basis of impotence. Consequently, such proceedings cannot be brought after the death of either partner by either an heir or a creditor. A person who married another with the knowledge of the other's impotence is not entitled to use the impotence as a basis for annulment proceedings.

The definition of impotence for annulment purposes is an incurable inability to *consummate the marriage,* that is, to perform the sex act, this condition having existed prior to the marriage. The inability is considered to be equivalent to incurable if it would take a serious operation to remedy the condition, or even a minor operation, which the afflicted party refuses to undergo.

The term impotence means the lack of capacity for complete sexual intercourse; being capable of partial intercourse only, is also deemed to be impotence. Thus, the male must be capable of complete penetration and the ejaculation of semen. If he has this capacity, the use of contraceptives or coitus interruptus does not affect the question of his potency.

A female is not necessarily impotent because she does not reach a climax. On the other hand, a woman's malformation makes a marriage voidable. Bearing a child is not an automatic sign of potence in such an instance, since conception can take place even through incomplete intercourse. Nor does fathering a child automatically stamp a man as potent, since *fecundation ab extra* may take place without penetration.

Impotence need not be caused by a biological incapacity. It is accepted as real if it is caused by nerves, or by an incurable hysterical condition, such as an invincible repugnance. Hysteria, which literally translated is *the woman's disease,* can also be suffered by men. The repugnance may well exist, not against the sex act in general, but against one's marriage partner in particular. If this is really the case, it is proper basis for an annulment.

As was stated in the definition, the impotence must have been in existence since before the time of the marriage. If impotence sets in after the marriage, it will not serve as grounds for an annulment. Nor will a marriage be annulled on the basis that a person is capable of intercourse, but wilfully refuses to consummate the marriage. Both these situations are grounds for annulment in England. The new Divorce Act makes some cases of impotence grounds for divorce in Canada. (*See* page 82.) After there has been a consummation of the marriage, the deliberate cessation of sexual intercouse might amount to cruelty and form a basis for a divorce on those grounds. (*See* page 79.)

Proof of Impotence. If a person denies that he is impotent, the burden to prove impotence is upon the spouse who alleged it. This can be attempted by a medical and/or psychiatric examination which is often inconclusive. The respondent might refuse to submit to the examination, but if he refuses, his conduct can be construed as evidence of his disability. Similarly, a person's wilful refusal to have sexual intercourse can be so construed. It is also regarded as evidence of impotence if a married woman is *virgo intacta.*

Impotence must not be confused with sterility, that is, the inability to father, or to bear a child, respectively. Sterility is not grounds for annulment.

BARS TO RELIEF

As in divorce cases, the court will investigate if there has been any collusion or connivance by the parties to the annulment proceedings. If the court finds this to have been the case, it will refuse to grant the desired decree.

DECREES NISI AND ABSOLUTE

If the court finds that a "marriage" is void *ab initio,* it issues an annulment *decree absolute,* without an intervening *decree nisi.* (*See* pages 45 and 95.) An exception exists in New Brunswick, where a *judgment nisi* precedes the final judgment by thirty days. When an annulment is based on the voidable grounds of impotence, a *decree nisi* has to precede the *decree absolute,* as in divorce cases, except in British Columbia and the Yukon (which had no *decrees nisi* at all before the passing of the new Divorce Act), and in Manitoba.

JURISDICTION

A Canadian petition for annulment of marriage can always be lodged in the court of the province in which the petitioner is *domiciled.* In addition, some courts have assumed authority to hear annulment cases where both the parties are *resident* in the jurisdiction, without either party necessarily having his domicile there. And some courts have felt similarly competent if the marriage was celebrated in their jurisdiction and one of the parties resides there.

While marriages and separations are governed by the laws of the province in which the couple resides, the question as to where a person is domiciled is of importance not only in annulment petitions, but also in connection with wills, inheritance, real estate, Estate Taxes and succession duties, and other legal topics. The new Divorce Act abolished provincial distinctions for divorce purposes, placing domicile on a Canada-wide basis.

DOMICILE

The concept of domicile (or domicil) is not necessarily the same as that of residence, whether temporary or permanent. Nor is the country in which a person is domiciled necessarily the country of which he is a national, a subject, or a citizen. Domicile is a combination of physical residence in a jurisdiction (which might be a country, a province, or a state) coupled with a state of mind: namely, the intention to stay in that jurisdiction permanently.

Domicile of Origin. Every child is born with a *domicile of* *origin,* that is, with the domicile which his father has at the time of the child's birth. If the child has no living father at the time of his birth, he becomes vested with his mother's domicile. A foundling is domiciled in the place of his birth.

While a person's nationality or citizenship is generally determinable by his passport, there is no document evidencing a person's domicile. It is not always an easy matter to determine a person's domicile, particularly if this problem is not brought up until after his death, as sometimes happens.

The question of a person's physical residence is usually determined with little difficulty, but the question of his intention may have to be proved by his actions and behaviour, in addition to his remarks. A person's statement regarding his intention to stay in a certain territory permanently, is not necessarily conclusive evidence of his intention, particularly if it was to his advantage to make such a statement at the time.

Domicile of Wife. Upon her marriage, a wife automatically acquires her husband's domicile. If he changes his domicile, her domicile and that of his dependent children is also changed automatically to his new domicile. This is true even when the husband and wife are separated. After the husband's death, or after a dissolution of the marriage, his wife retains his domicile, until she establishes another domicile of her own. If the children are fatherless, they follow their mother's domicile.

Domicile of Choice. It is quite possible for a person to change his domicile from his domicile of origin to a new one, called his *domicile of choice.* This happens by moving to another jurisdiction *and* by forming the intention to stay there permanently. Until *both* these steps have been taken, a person retains his domicile of origin. (A lunatic cannot change his domicile, since he lacks the ability to form the necessary intention.) To establish whether a change of domicile has taken place, let us use two examples.

An illustration of one extreme might be the case of an immigrant to Canada who has accumulated wealth in his new country. He has a prosperous business and lives with his family in a nicely furnished home which he owns. His children have been born in this country and they only speak English. He frequently expresses his admiration for this country. However, such a person may not be domiciled in Canada, if it can be proved that he ultimately plans to return to "the old country" after retirement, for example, by buying a house there.

On the other hand, an immigrant might acquire a new domicile the moment he lands in Canada. He has physically arrived in the new territory and his intention to stay permanently might be proved by the following:

- Obtaining an immigration visa,
- Liquidating his business and personal affairs in his previous domicile,
- Giving up a club membership,
- Moving his furniture and his family,
- Becoming a naturalized citizen,
- Changing his name, or even
- Buying a burial plot.

Change of Domicile of Choice. A person can change his domicile more than once. Someone who had his domicile of origin in Northern Ireland, for example, may have changed it to the province of Ontario by following the process just described. If he decides to move from Ontario to Buffalo, New York, permanently, he, along with his wife and children, acquires New York State domicile the moment he crosses into New York State, even if his family does not accompany him at that time.

This situation illustrates a simple case of a man changing from one domicile of choice (Ontario) to another domicile of choice (New York). It becomes a little more complicated when a man leaves his domicile of choice (New York) in order to live permanently in Florida, for example. The moment he leaves New York State, he loses his New York domicile and his domicile of origin (Northern Ireland) re-attaches to him temporarily. When he reaches Florida safely, he acquires a third domicile of choice in Florida. Should he die en route to Florida, the laws of Northern Ireland will govern his affairs.

A similar situation arises if he decides to leave Florida because he has heard British Columbia is so wonderful. He gives up his Florida apartment, stores his furniture, and goes to British Columbia for a year to see if he likes it there. He loses his Florida domicile the moment he leaves the state and reverts to his Northern Ireland domicile of origin. This he keeps even after his arrival in British Columbia where he does not attain a domicile until he makes a definite decision to settle in British Columbia permanently.

Wife's Domicile. A woman who seeks an annulment on

grounds rendering the marriage void *ab initio,* can petition for annulment in the province where she has her independent domicile. This procedure is based on the reasoning that, not being validly married, she is technically unmarried and, therefore, she has a domicile of her own which is not necessarily that of her husband's.

On the other hand, a wife who desires a declaration of nullity on the voidable grounds of impotence, is married to her husband until the nullity decree is issued. Consequently, she bears her husband's domicile until then and, if she wishes to institute proceedings in the province of her domicile, she must do so in the province where her husband is domiciled.

CONFLICT OF LAWS

All previously stated rules concerning domicile are the English ones, in effect throughout the Common Law areas of the world. The rules of domicile are not, necessarily, the same in other countries. If they conflict with our laws, there are certain rules of Private International Law which regulate the discrepancies.

If matrimonial proceedings are brought in a Canadian court, in which a person is involved whose place of domicile is in dispute, then the Canadian court will determine his place of domicile according to Canadian rules. (The same rule also applies, *mutatis mutandis,* in most other countries.) If the Canadian court determines this person to have a foreign domicile, it will employ the foreign matrimonial laws to decide upon the validity of his marriage, divorce, etc., provided the foreign laws are not repugnant to our sense of morality.

Foreign Divorces. Consequently, foreign divorces do have validity in Canada if a person, whom a Canadian court has found to be domiciled in a foreign state, obtained a divorce in that state according to its laws.

If the person is found by our courts to have a Canadian domicile, then his case will be decided according to Canadian law. According to a foreign territory's laws, this person may also have a domicile there. In this case, the Canadian court will still apply Canadian law and disregard the foreign laws. It is for this reason that our courts seldom respect divorces granted to persons in those states of the U.S. or Mexico, which regard him as domiciled there on grounds we consider very flimsy, such as a mere six-week residence.

Foreign Marriages. With regard to the validity of marriages which have been performed in Canada for persons who are domiciled elsewhere, it seems established that our courts will regard as valid a marriage which complied with the Canadian requirements, even if any foreign rules regarding the *form* of the marriage were violated.

However, if the foreign jurisdiction declares certain marriages of people domiciled there invalid because of something more fundamental than form, such as an incapacity, then our courts will respect that foreign law. Consequently, if a person who is domiciled in England goes through the marriage ceremony here while either he or his partner is under sixteen years of age, the marriage will be held void by our courts, because it violates English law, even if such a marriage may not be considered illegal in the territory of its solemnization.

Similarly, a marriage will be regarded as void by our courts, if it violates the rules regarding consanguinity in the country in which the party to the marriage is domiciled. For example, the marriage of cousins might be illegal in that country, while our laws regard it as legal.

Our courts will recognize as valid a marriage which is performed in another country if it complies with the marriage formalities of that country, even though they differ from the formalities required by our laws, for example, a marriage by proxy. In fact, our courts may recognize a marriage as binding if the country in which it was performed has less stringent consanguinity laws than ours, for example, a marriage between an uncle and his niece, provided both parties to the marriage have their domicile in that foreign country.

chapter 6

THE TRADITIONAL DIVORCE GROUNDS

The traditional grounds for divorce are the so-called matrimonial offences. Marriage, as was seen earlier, is a special kind of contract, whereby certain rights and obligations are imposed on the parties to it. For example, there is a mutual undertaking to love, support and assist one another, and it is the socially accepted setting for the bearing and raising of children.

If one of the parties to the marriage violates some of these contract terms, the other becomes entitled to demand a termination of the contract. In other words, he may sue for a divorce on the grounds of the other's breach of contract. If the court is satisfied that the wrongdoer has committed the alleged offence, it orders a dissolution of the marriage. The wronged party may or may not sue at his option. If he fails to do so, the marriage remains in existence, technically. Normally, the wrongdoer cannot sue for divorce; however, the new Divorce Act allows a deserter to obtain his freedom in some very closely supervised circumstances. (*See* chapter 7.)

ADULTERY

Ours is a monogamous society, and it is an essential part of the marriage ceremony that the couple undertake to be true to each other exclusively. If either spouse strays from the path of marital fidelity, the other acquires the immediate right to a divorce. Adultery strikes at the roots of marriage so fundamentally, that it has been grounds for divorce, ever since our courts began to grant divorces. One isolated act of adultery entitles the wronged party to put an end to the marriage. If the marriage is sufficiently sound otherwise, it is open to the wronged spouse to ignore the incident. Whether or not he wants to do this, is the individual's decision. There are no statistics to show how many divorces are instituted on the basis of an isolated digression from the straight and narrow path, or in how many cases the act of adultery complained of is the final straw which breaks the proverbial camel's back.

Until 1968, adultery was just about the only reason for which a divorce could be obtained. For the sake of completeness, the other reasons were unnatural sexual offences and, in Nova Scotia, cruelty. These marital offences continue to be grounds for divorce under the new Divorce Act and will, therefore, be discussed in detail.

While it is likely that adultery will become less and less important as grounds for divorce, it is still very popular with lawyers. Divorce lawyers have used it for years. They have become familiar with its technicalities; and that they are loth to abandon it in favour of other divorce grounds is shown by the fact that, in Toronto, 120 divorce petitions were filed under the old procedures during the week before the new divorce laws came into effect on July 2, 1968.

Naturally, numerous divorce cases will still be brought on the basis of adultery. But, it can be stated with a fair degree of assurance, that any adultery which is claimed in the future, will be genuine. That this has not always been the case in the past is so well known in the legal profession that it hardly merits mention. This is not to say that lawyers have acted dishonestly or unethically, for it is not a lawyer's responsibility to cross-examine his client intensively regarding the truth of the facts which his client lays before him in connection with the alleged adultery. The lawyer is entitled to assume that his client will not perjure himself, and provided the lawyer has taken reasonable safeguards to verify the truth of the client's statements, he cannot technically be blamed if his client has duped him. It is the responsibility of the presiding judge, and sometimes that of an official called the Queen's Proctor, to uncover false or fabricated evidence, and cases of collusion and connivance. (*See* page 64.)

The previous assertions should not be suspected of sensation-mongering. During the passage of Divorce Bill No. 187 through Parliament, Mr. Andrew Brewin, the M.P. for Greenwood and a lawyer by profession, made the unequivocal statement that, when adultery was virtually the only grounds for divorce, many cases of adultery occurred which otherwise might not have taken place. In other words, evidence was deliberately fabricated to furnish grounds for divorce and, by making the customary declaration in the witness box that the evidence was bona fide and not a fabrication, the grave offence of perjury was committed also.

According to Mr. Arnold Peters, the MP. for Temiskaming, actual adultery took place in only about ten per cent of the divorce cases based on adultery. The others were fictitious. There are certain unscrupulous individuals (every once in a while, their activities are uncovered by an alert judge) who set up "a neat little divorce package" for a standard fee. It works like this: A hotel room is rented; the husband (who usually plays the part of the adulterer in this tragi-comedy) checks in with a woman who has been supplied by the "divorce agent", and signs the register as *Mr. & Mrs.* Frequently his pen runs out of ink at that moment, or some other little stratagem is employed to make sure the desk clerk remembers their faces. The couple order breakfast from room service the next morning, and they always ensure being seen in a double bed together. It is almost routine for the coffee to be spilled to make the waiter remember them better. It is quite safe to assume that this is the full extent of the physical association between the couple in bed.

At the divorce hearing, the desk clerk and the waiter will be asked to look at the petitioning wife and at a photograph of her respondent husband. They will recognize the husband as the man who spent the night in their hotel, but they will not recognize his real wife, thus proving that the husband was at the hotel with another woman.

Many men refuse to degrade themselves by participating in such a farce and prefer to commit outright perjury. According to Mr. Peters, in a study of 1400 divorce cases involving adultery, 400 of the people named as respondents were completely non-existent, and the addresses given for them were fictitious.

Definition. The definition of adultery is "voluntary sexual intercourse with any person of the opposite sex, other than one's spouse." According to other definitions, adultery can be committed only by a married person. This distinction is of no practical consequence in divorce proceedings, since an unmarried person cannot get divorced, anyway.

Sexual intercourse does not constitute adultery if it is not voluntary. Consequently, a wife who has been raped or otherwise forced to have intercourse by serious threats is not deemed to have committed adultery; nor, if she has been drugged, hypnotized, or tricked into it by a person impersonating her husband, or by some pseudo-medical quack claiming to give her therapy.

To constitute adultery, it is essential for sexual intercourse to have taken place; anything short of that is not adultery. It is still considered to be adultery if there has been but a slight penetration, even without the hymen being ruptured. Consequently, being a *virgo intacta* is not automatically proof that there has been no adultery. This condition raises a strong assumption of innocence, of course, which it will take a substantial amount of contrary evidence to rebut.

Proof of Adultery. Any allegation which a party to a law suit makes in court must be proved by him to the satisfaction of the court according to the established rules of evidence. If a divorce petition is based on the respondent's alleged adultery, and the defence to the action is a denial of the adultery, then the commission of the adultery must be proved. No case need ever be proved to the hilt. Even in criminal prosecutions it is sufficient to prove that the accused committed the alleged crime "beyond a reasonable doubt"; not, beyond the shadow of a doubt. In Canadian divorce cases, it is not necessary to go even that far. It suffices to prove that a "balance of probabilities" exists that the adultery, or other matrimonial offence, has been committed.

There is certainly no need to produce *direct evidence* of the offence; for example, a witness's testimony that he saw the adultery being committed. If that were the requirement, then no divorces would ever be granted. Adequate *circumstantial evidence* is perfectly acceptable, as it is in criminal cases also. Adultery can be proved in many ways. Generally, adultery is adequately proved if the respondent has shown undue familiarity with the co-respondent, and had the opportunity to commit adultery.

By "undue familiarity" is meant something more than an ordinary sign of friendship, such as a brief handholding, normally close dancing, whispering, an innocent pat, or even an occasional kiss.

By "opportunity" is meant being together in privacy for lengthy stretches of time, particularly at night. Being found in bed together is usually conclusive evidence of adultery. Also, when a couple who have previously displayed undue familiarity, spend an entire night together alone in a room, it can be presumed that adultery has been committed unless there is a convincing explanation to the contrary.

The following explanation which a married woman gave in an Ontario case in 1967 was not considered a convincing one. Mrs. Brown, who was judicially separated from her husband, spent the night in her apartment with a gentleman friend of long standing, under the following circumstances: She claimed that she was on the verge of a nervous breakdown because she knew her husband was outside the house watching her. She explained that her married friend stayed with her until dawn merely to calm her. The appeal court disbelieved her statement that the lights were left on in her apartment and drew the inference that adultery had been committed.

Private Detectives. If a spouse is suspected of infidelity which he will not admit, it is common practice for the person seeking the divorce, to engage the services of a reputable firm of investigators, the so-called private detectives. The investigator, who must be government licenced and bonded in most of the provinces, will first try to uncover some evidence of past adultery. If he is unsuccessful in this, he will place the suspect under surveillance, to try to catch him *in flagrante delicto.* It is not unusual for the operator to be accompanied on his shadowing tour by one, or preferably two, non-professionals, for example, two friends of the prospective petitioner. The reason for this precaution is that the evidence which an investigator gives in court is sometimes regarded with suspicion since it is obviously to the advantage of the investigator's professional reputation if his clients generally win their cases. His evidence might, accordingly, be considered a shade less impartial than that of the independent witnesses who can corroborate his observations.

If the observed conduct of the suspect is on the borderline of being apparently reprehensible or possibly innocent, the operator will frequently attempt to obtain corroborative evidence in the form of other past misconduct or immorality on the suspect's part.

Brothels. A visit by a woman to a brothel (whether as a staff member or as a customer) is regarded as conclusive evidence of her adultery. A similar visit by a man is strong, but not irrebuttable evidence of his adultery.

V.D. The respondent's affliction with venereal disease is evidence of his having committed adultery, provided he was free of the disease before the marriage, and provided the petitioning spouse does not suffer from the same disease. It might be possible for the respondent to prove, however, that the venereal disease was the delayed outbreak of a case which had been latent or dormant since long before the marriage; or, if the disease was acquired after the marriage, that it was acquired innocently.

Non-Access. A court will presume that a wife committed adultery if she bears a child in spite of the fact her husband has been proven sterile; or, if the husband could not have been with his wife at the time the conception allegedly took place because of his absence or because of a legal separation between them. To support this charge, the husband may try to produce expert blood test evidence to disprove his paternity. The fact that contraceptives were used in the marriage is not regarded as relevant.

While the normal gestation period for a full-term child is 270-280 days, the courts give every consideration to the possibility of variations in the norm. The courts have accepted medical evidence to the effect that it is quite possible for a normal child to be born 224 days after conception. In other decided cases, the courts have accepted the possibility of a premature child being born in 174 days and, in an extreme case, of a child being born after 352 days. In a case where a child was born 360 days after the alleged date of conception, the birth was held to constitute evidence of adultery.

If the woman tries to conceal the birth of her child from her husband after his return, the birth can be proved by an entry in the Register of Births which was made by her, or by the child's natural father.

Bigamy. Under the new Divorce Act, a person can be divorced by his spouse if he bigamously marries somebody else. Before the new law came into effect, it was not automatically assumed that actual adultery accompanied the bigamy. However, if the bigamist confessed to the adultery in his trial, or if he pleaded "guilty" when charged with the crime of bigamy, this was considered sufficient evidence of his adultery with his new "spouse". Parliament, incidentally, granted divorces after any convictions for bigamy in cases lodged before it.

UNDEFENDED CASES

The preceding cases illustrated legal actions in which the respondent denied having committed adultery. There are many more cases, however, which are undefended, where the respondent is willing to admit his adultery, because he probably wants his freedom as much as the petitioner does.

Even in these undefended cases, it is necessary to produce satisfactory evidence of the alleged adultery, not in order to overcome the respondent's denial of it, but in order to satisfy the court that the adultery was genuinely committed. There are many cases where adultery is deliberately committed for the sole purpose of furnishing grounds for divorce, and there are other cases where the alleged adultery is entirely fictitious. (*See* page 59.) In both these instances, the court refuses to grant a divorce and it might, in fact, institute proceedings against the person who tried to mislead the court. He might be charged with perjury or contempt of court or be penalized by the revocation of certain licences he may hold.

CORROBORATION

It is for this reason that the respondent's confession that he has committed adultery is seldom accepted as sufficient evidence of adultery, unless the confession is corroborated by other evidence, such as being seen in bed with the co-respondent or by evidence of having spent the night with an unduly close friend.

While evidence as to one's own adultery is frequently given voluntarily, it is a court rule that no party or witness to a divorce action may be asked questions about any adultery he may have committed, without his first having consented to such a questioning. Today it is permissible, contrary to previous usage, for a parent to give evidence which will *bastardize his child.* For example, a husband can give evidence to prove his own *non-access* to his wife during the critical period thereby proving that some other man was the father of the child to which his wife gave birth during wedlock. Such a child, incidentally, is legally regarded as a legitimate child.

In genuine cases of adultery, the guilty party frequently lives *common law* with another person. In such cases, the standard procedure to furnish proof of the adultery is for a visitor to their home to testify that he saw evidence of the couple living together as man and wife; for example, that there was only one bed in the only bedroom and that their clothes occupied the same closet. Frequently, the person who gives this evidence is the process server, who served the divorce petition on the respondent. Adultery is just about conclusive if the common law "wife" uses her man's surname for her own or if she has given birth to a child while living with him.

BARS TO RELIEF

Collusion. If the court comes to the conclusion, from its own observation or after receiving a report from the Queen's Proctor, that the divorce evidence was deliberately fabricated or facilitated by the husband and wife acting *in collusion,* a divorce decree will be refused, as will also an order for annulment or judicial separation. The Queen's Proctor can be a permanent official, or he can be appointed *ad hoc* to investigate one particular case, or his functions can be exercised by another official, such as the Attorney General of Nova Scotia. *Collusion* is defined in the new Act, in summary, as "an agreement, understanding, arrangement, or conspiracy to which the petitioner is a party, for the purpose of subverting justice, by fabricating or suppressing evidence, or otherwise to deceive the court."

A typical example of collusion is a petitioner's offer to compensate his spouse for manufacturing divorce evidence, either by outright payment, or by a willingness to forgo all claims to maintenance and custody of the children. However, asking the other party to supply particulars and evidence of an act of adultery which has already been committed, or offering to supply the other party with such particulars, is not collusion; unless a high price, amounting to a bribe, is offered or a large amount, amounting to extortion, is charged for this information. It is not considered collusion for a respondent husband to offer to make reasonable, even generous, provision for his wife if she consents to divorce him, or for them to conduct preliminary discussions regarding the division of their property or the future of their children after the contemplated divorce.

In summary, it is not necessarily regarded as collusion that both parties desire the divorce; that one party requests the other to commence proceedings against him; or that one party furnishes the other with existing evidence against himself. What must not be done, is to make an attempt to deceive the court. If the parties have come to any financial arrangements, for example, regarding the amount to be paid for the other's maintenance, bearing or sharing court costs of the divorce action, or to arrangements concerning the future of the children, particulars must be supplied to the court so that it may decide for itself whether the arrangements involved indicate collusive conduct or not.

A recent case to illustrate these points took place in Saskatchewan in 1965. There, an action was not regarded as collusive, even though the respondent, a Mrs. Peel, offered to pay the full court costs if her husband would sue for divorce, so that she could legalize her common law association with the co-respondent.

To avoid doing or saying anything which might be interpreted as collusion, it is wise to let one's experienced divorce lawyer thresh out all preliminary negotiations of this nature with the other party's lawyer. For example, the lawyer might draft a letter for a petitioning wife to write to her guilty husband, asking him to supply her with the necessary divorce evidence but avoiding any reference to the lawyer's participation for various reasons. An interesting point in this connection is that it is the petitioner's duty to do the best she can to find out from her husband the name of the *co-respondent* (the "woman in the case"). (*See* page 93.) If the husband is unwilling to supply her name, the wife must, on no account, enter into an agreement with him to stop trying to find out the woman's name. If she is unsuccessful in finding out her name, the wife's chances of obtaining the divorce are by no means defeated. If all the other circumstances warrant it, she will be granted the divorce. The extent of the wife's obligation in this case is just to do her best to *try* to obtain the co-respondent's name.

If the court dismisses a divorce petition on the grounds of collusion, there is nothing except the expense and the delay to prevent another non-collusive action from being brought on the basis of the same evidence as in the first action.

Connivance. In the case of the *matrimonial offences* of adultery, unnatural sexual offences, bigamy and cruelty, a divorce will be refused if the petitioner has *connived at* the respondent's offence. In its discretion the court may, nevertheless, grant a divorce if it believes the public interest to be better served thereby. Connivance is committed by "assenting to, aiding, or encouraging the offence in question, or by acquiescing expressly, or tacitly, in the continuance of an adulterous association he knows to exist."

Thus, if one spouse deliberately, with his emotions under control, invites or permits the other to engage in extra-marital relations, or if two couples commit a wife-swap, the resulting adultery cannot be used as valid grounds for divorce.

Also, if the one spouse, knowing the other to be half-inclined to be unfaithful, throws temptation his way and deliberately provides the opportunity for adultery, then the ensuing adultery will have been connived at and will not warrant a divorce. Similarly, if the one spouse is aware that the other is about to commit adultery, and deliberately turns a blind eye to this without making any attempts to prevent it, he loses his legal rights of redress.

Decisions have varied in cases where a husband concealed himself in order to witness his wife's anticipated adultery. Slight differences in the accompanying circumstances resulted in a divorce being granted in the one case, but being refused on the grounds of connivance in the other case. The court would be inclined to be suspicious of cases, sometimes reported from the United States, where a photographer was conveniently present to record the adultery.

Not belonging in the category of connivance is the person who has a naive overconfidence in the faithfulness of his spouse and is guilty of stupidity, rather than intrigue, in granting too much leeway to the other's wayward tendencies.

It is not regarded as connivance if the petitioner reluctantly tolerates an adulterous relationship which he knows to exist, and which he has been unsuccessful in stopping. In illustration, a Mr. Bowen was granted a divorce in a 1966 Ontario appeal case under the following circumstances:

After Mr. and Mrs. Bowen had entered into a separation agreement, Mr. Bowen moved out of the family apartment while Mrs. Bowen continued to live there. Mr. Bowen continued paying the apartment rent for one month thereafter, even though he knew that another man had moved in with Mrs. Bowen, and that they were living there as man and wife. On appeal, Mr. Bowen was found not to have been guilty of connivance at the continuance of his wife's adultery.

Condonation. As in the case of connivance, the court will refuse to grant the petitioner a divorce (unless it would be in the better public interest to order otherwise) if, with knowledge of the circumstances, he has forgiven his spouse the matrimonial offence on which the action is based. *Condonation* takes place by forgiveness **and** by the resumption of cohabitation. Cohabitation need not, necessarily, be coupled with sexual intercourse, though the resumption of intercourse naturally raises a strong presumption of an intention to forgive.

Cohabitation consists of deliberately living together as husband and wife. The occasional meeting, even if associated with sexual intercourse, is not necessarily regarded as a resumption of cohabitation amounting to condonation. In fact, the new Divorce Act specifically permits one three-month trial period of resumed cohabitation for the purpose of attempting a reconciliation, without this constituting condonation. It should be remembered that a three-month period of this nature does not serve to interrupt desertion either.

It is for this reason that, when a petitioner in the witness box is asked the standard question by the judge whether he has forgiven the respondent his offence, the standard answer is "no". Everybody in the courtroom knows full well that the petitioner, though he might have the most forgiving nature in the world, has previously been instructed by his lawyer about the technical significance of the word *forgiveness*.

Condonation consists of outright forgiveness, without any conditions attached. If a wife grants condonation to her husband on condition, for example, that he stop playing poker or going to girlie shows, her condonation will not be voided by his breaking his promises to that effect. Under the new Act, a matrimonial offence of any nature, once it has been fully condoned, can no longer be revived by any subsequent misbehaviour of the respondent's, not even by a matrimonial offence, as it could previously.

If condonation takes place at any time before the issue of the *decree absolute*, no divorce will be granted, even if the court has already pronounced a *decree nisi*.

OTHER MATRIMONIAL OFFENCES

Ever since divorces have been granted by the English courts, a husband could be divorced if he committed *rape, sodomy,* or *bestiality*. Alberta and Saskatchewan grant judicial separations if the last two offences are even attempted, but a divorce is granted only if the offence is actually committed.

Rape is committed when a man forces a woman by violence,

or the threat of violence, to have sexual intercourse with him, of however slight a nature. For divorce purposes, it is not rape to commit the serious crime of *statutory rape*, that is, to have sexual intercourse with a girl under sixteen years of age (or older, under certain circumstances), even though she freely consented to it. Normally, a man cannot commit the crime of rape against his wife, although this is possible if the husband and wife are legally separated.

Buggery can consist either of *bestiality*, which is an unnatural offence committed by a male with animals, or of *sodomy*, which consists of anal intercourse by a male with any person including his wife.

All these acts are crimes, of course; but, as with bigamy, a conviction in a criminal court for any of these crimes is not sufficient evidence of the commission of the matrimonial offence at the divorce trial, unless the accused had confessed, or pleaded guilty at his earlier criminal trial.

If a wife gives her true consent to the unnatural acts being practiced upon her, she cannot successfully claim a divorce on that basis. It should be remembered also that cruelty is no grounds for matrimonial relief if the victim consents to it. The consent in question must not be obtained by force or by trickery, such as by convincing a naive young wife that practices of such a nature are normal among married couples.

DAMAGES FOR ADULTERY

Financial arrangements which are made between divorced couples and the orders which the court makes regarding payments by one ex-spouse to the other are discussed in chapter nine. At this point, it is appropriate to set out the proceedings which can be taken by the innocent party against a third party who contributed toward the foundering of the marriage.

CRIMINAL CONVERSATION

This activity neither concerns the commission of a crime, nor does it involve a verbal exchange of ideas, as the title might imply. *Criminal conversation* is an old-fashioned term signifying the commission of adultery with a man's wife and entitling a husband to damages against the man who defiled his wife. This particular action has been replaced in England by a claim for damages against the co-respondent, which is part and parcel of a divorce action. This is also true in the western Canadian provinces. However, the old separate action still survives in Ontario and the Maritimes, although, in practice, it could be and customarily was, joined with the principal divorce action with the leave of the court. Under the new rules, it becomes the subject of a separate action in Ontario; but the court may grant leave for the two actions to be tried concurrently. (*See* page 93.)

ENTICEMENT

While *crim. con.*, as it was once familiarly called by lawyers, could be likened to a tort action for trespass to property, so *enticement* is not unlike the tort of deliberately and maliciously inducing someone to commit a breach of contract. Enticement is committed, by either a man or a woman, by luring someone away from his spouse so that he is deprived of the other's *consortium*, consisting of companionship, affection, household responsibilities, etc. Although rarely done, this action can be brought independently of divorce proceedings. In practice, it is tried concurrently with a divorce action with the leave of the court, if it is claimed at all.

This type of action will fail if:

- The defendant was unaware that his friend was married, or
- It was not the defendant's intention, or actions, that destroyed the marriage, or
- The defendant induced his friend to leave the spouse for no selfish reasons, but for the friend's best interests, or
- The parties were already previously separated, or
- The couple continued to live together in spite of the defendant's activities.

ALIENATION OF AFFECTIONS

This type of action, by a man or a woman, has ceased to have a separate existence. If the defendant can be shown responsible for alienating one spouse's affections from the other in an action for *criminal conversation* or *enticement*, the damages awarded against him will be correspondingly higher.

Since many of today's divorce cases are undefended, it is unusual for damages to be claimed against a co-respondent. But, if damages are claimed and awarded in a criminal conversation or enticement action, they will be based not only on the degree to which the third party was responsible for the adultery, but also in accordance with his wealth. The reasons for this are that his wealth and social standing were possibly lures to the enticement and that the punishment should be a truly effective one.

Seduction. It may be of interest to note that the head of a household may sue for damages a man who has *seduced* his daughter or any unmarried female living "under his protection."

From the previous statements, and those in connection with judicial separations, a person contemplating an affair with someone else's spouse should be able to work out for himself a fairly accurate picture of the consequences.

FATAL ACCIDENTS ACT

If a person is injured through someone else's fault, he can naturally sue him for the damages caused by the negligence or other tort. But, if he dies as a consequence of the "accident", his surviving spouse or other dependent relative can sue the guilty party for the loss caused by the death. The damages are usually based on an estimate of the capitalized value of the deceased's lost earnings over his normal life expectancy. Beyond this, there is no compensation for the loss of a deceased or injured spouse's *consortium*.

WORKMEN'S COMPENSATION

Completing the discussion of a dependent person's rights after the death of his spouse, mention should be made of the Workmen's Compensation Acts existing in all the provinces. These Acts provide not only for free medical treatment and substantial payments to workers who have been disabled by accident or industrial disease while at work (for example, up to 75% of $7000 a year for a totally disabled worker in Ontario, free of income tax); they also provide for payments for such a person's surviving spouse (a $500 lump sum and $125 per month) and dependent children ($50 per month for each) in the case of his death. In Ontario, a permanent common law union is regarded as equivalent to a legal marriage in this connection.

The benefits continue for the rest of the surviving spouse's life, unless she remarries in which case she is paid a lump sum, amounting to two years' payment. A common law partner's benefits end when she marries or enters another union. A "legal" widow's benefits also end if she enters an irregular union and the Workmen's Compensation Board finds out about it.

chapter 7

THE NEW DIVORCE LAWS: GROUNDS FOR DIVORCE

HISTORY

As mentioned earlier, our divorce laws have been in effect, virtually unchanged, for almost a century. Since 1870, the only changes of any consequence were the following:

- In 1925, the *double standard* for men and women was removed, meaning that, from then on, women had to prove nothing beyond adultery on their husbands' part to secure a divorce. Previously, they had to adduce additional grounds, such as rape, incest, cruelty, desertion, etc., coupled with his adultery; while a petitioning husband had to prove nothing but his wife's adultery.
- In 1930, women who had been deserted for two years were allowed to start divorce proceedings (on the grounds of the husband's adultery) in the province in which they were themselves domiciled, instead of in the province where the deserting husband had established his new domicile.

BRITISH REFORM

The reform of the divorce laws has long been a matter of great public interest in the English common law areas. *A Bill of Divorcement*, a 1921 play on this topic by Clemence Dane, enjoyed a long run on the British and American stages. In the movie version, John Barrymore starred dramatically as the husband gone insane, to whom his wife continued to be tied in marital bonds.

A famous writer for *Punch*, A. P. Herbert, had two axes to grind persistently: the stupidity of the English drinking laws and the need for reform of the divorce laws. In 1934, he wrote a best seller, *Holy Deadlock,* in which he highlighted the indignities of fabricated evidence and perjury to which unfortunate, yet fundamentally decent, people had to stoop in order to secure a divorce under the law as it then stood. Herbert (now Sir Alan) ran for Parliament as a Liberal member for Oxford University and was elected on his first attempt. He introduced a private member's bill for divorce reform and won the distinction of being just about the first freshman member to have his bill considered, and actually converted into law in 1937. Basically, it added cruelty, three years' desertion, and five years' insanity as divorce grounds.

New Zealand began liberalizing its divorce laws in 1920, Scotland in 1938, Australia in 1959, and New York (though no longer a British colony) in 1967. In Europe, the Scandinavian countries are leaders in the field of modernized divorce laws.

CANADIAN REFORM

Over the years, many members of Canadian Parliament have tried to introduce private bills for divorce reform (for example, Senator Walter M. Aseltine in 1938 and 1955), but none of them was successful. Finally, in March of 1966, a special Joint Committee of both Houses of Parliament, under the co-chairmanship of (ninety-year "young") Senator Arthur W. Roebuck, Q.C. and Mr. A. J. P. Cameron, Q.C., M.P., was appointed to examine the question, soon after Senator Roebuck had introduced yet another divorce reform bill in the Senate. Mr. E. Russell Hopkins, Law Clerk and Parliamentary Counsel of the Senate started the ball rolling with the following words on June 28, 1966:

"This planet has turned on its axis many times since 1857 when the grounds for divorce in most Canadian provinces were established. I might add that the present law of divorce in Canada is a curious and somewhat delicate mosaic which has been adjusted from time to time in a piecemeal, pragmatic and perhaps, typically Anglo-Saxon manner, and that any further improvement in its design will require not only a steady hand but a fine chisel indeed. There will be needed also a sort of liquid cement compounded of caution and confidence in equal parts."

After many meetings, a profound study of the divorce laws

of other legal systems, and perusing the briefs of over seventy individuals, churches, and other organizations, they made their report with about twenty-one recommendations in June 1967, at a cost of $82,000. With very few changes from these recommendations, Minister of Justice Pierre Elliott Trudeau introduced a bill into Parliament for the reform of our divorce laws the following December. On the 19th of the same month, this was passed by the Commons (with negligible amendments) and by the Senate the following January to become the Divorce Act, 1968. It was labelled a Christmas present for the 500,000 persons estimated by the Canadian Bar Association as being virtually forced "to live common law" under the existing laws.

PASSAGE THROUGH PARLIAMENT

Upon introduction of the bill in Parliament Mr. Trudeau, although chivvied by Members with being a bachelor and a "swinger" was congratulated for his initiative in tackling a subject which had long been regarded as a sacred cow. Not only did he receive the approval of Robert Stanfield, the Leader of the Opposition, but also of other members of Parliament, some of whom, however, did not subsequently hesitate to press vigorously for amendments: notably Mr. Andrew Brewin and Mr. Robert McCleave, both members of the original Joint Committee.

In the course of his remarks, the Minister stated that it had become necessary to bring the law more into line with the present social climate, while leaving the family surrounded with maximum protection, and to achieve the desired reform without violating or offending federal-provincial relationships. On the second reading of the bill, the Minister admitted, when it was put to him, that many marriages would not break down if poverty, slums, alcoholism, etc., were removed, but he pleaded that everything could not be attended to at once. Pending the elimination of these basic ills, a beginning could at least be made by curing the symptoms. He also admitted that the bill as it now stood, was not necessarily perfect; for example, some of the time elements included in it were based on nothing but intelligent guesswork. But he felt it was of greatest benefit to all concerned to pass the bill into law without further delay, and to make amendments subsequently, as they become necessary and desirable. Although he had been eager to include further improvements to the existing law, these require the approval of the individual provinces first. This approval will be sought in a planned series of meetings with the provincial Chief Justices and government officials such as the Attorneys-General over an indeterminate future time. As a matter of fact, five months (instead of the usual three) between the Assent to the Act and its coming into force were provided for, to allow the provinces to add their suggestions and to bring their own regulations into line with the new legislation.

THEORIES AND PRINCIPLES

It was stressed by the Minister that the new law is designed not only to make divorce easier, but to salvage marriages wherever possible. This latter purpose is considered at least as important as giving a legal burial to marriages which have died. As will be seen, the Act specifically requires the involved lawyers and the court to seek to reconcile the parties, so that the law can properly be called not only a divorce Act, but also a reconciliation Act.

The new law does more than extend the marital offences upon which to sue for divorce. It introduces the concept of a permanent marriage breakdown, one of the first on this continent to do so. This concept was the one which a study group, organized by the Archbishop of Canterbury, recommended in 1966 in a report entitled *Putting Asunder*, as being the only grounds for dissolving a marriage. This was also the view expressed to the Parliamentary Joint Committee in a combined brief of all the major Canadian churches and advocated throughout the passage of the bill by Mr. Brewin.

The new law has not, however, swung completely from the old principle of marital offences to this new concept of marriage breakdown. It is a composite Act, recognizing not only marital offences (where, theoretically, the one party's guilt merits punishment) but also numerous situations which result in a marriage disintegrating through no fault, necessarily, of one person in particular. The consequence of this is that divorce need no longer be considered a dirty word. The reason given for not swinging over completely to the new principle was, that it would place "too broad, undefined and uncontrolled discretion" in the hands of a judge whose duty it is to decide when a marriage has actually broken down, and that more uniformity in the granting of divorces could be achieved if Parliament spelled out fairly definitely the exact grounds on which a marriage should be considered as having broken down.

INNOVATIONS

Other innovations of the new Act provide for the following:

- A woman is given the same rights as a man regarding domicile, for obtaining a divorce in Canada or abroad. (*See* page 91.)
- Provision is made for the enforcement of court orders with regard to alimony, maintenance, and the custody of children, throughout all the provinces of Canada. (*See* page 91.)
- Divorce procedure for the residents of Quebec and Newfoundland is simplified. (*See* page 89.)

While there seems little doubt in the mind of our jurists that the British North America Act empowers the federal government to legislate on the topic of judicial separation, Ottawa feels reluctant to pass a federal law which might change the law of those provinces which have legislation of their own in this field. It is expected, however, that the relative importance of judicial separation will decrease substantially henceforth, since the new grounds for divorce are actually wider than the existing grounds for judicial separation in most provinces.

Nor does the new federal Act make provision for *separate maintenance*, that is, a final division of property among the divorced parties. This has again been avoided deliberately, so as not to conflict with the existing laws of the various provinces in this regard.

ADULTERY

Although many new grounds for divorce have been added by the new Act, the old grounds for divorce have not been abolished. Either husband or wife can still petition for divorce on the grounds of the other's isolated act of adultery (or cruelty in Nova Scotia) and the husband can still be divorced for his sodomy, bestiality, or rape. So can the wife, under the new Act. This is not as absurd as it sounds, since she can be guilty of these crimes technically by aiding and abetting a man to commit these acts. These terms have not been defined any further in the Act, since their meanings have been sufficiently well established in many past decisions. To constitute grounds for divorce, these offences must have been actually committed, not merely attempted.

HOMOSEXUALITY

Three new divorce offences have been created, becoming grounds for "instant divorce". (Instant to the extent that, at the time of writing, it takes about a year for a divorce hearing to come up before the courts in Toronto.) One of these offences consists of either the husband or wife "engaging in a homosexual act" since the marriage. This is not elaborated upon any further in the Act. Many other terms were defined but vaguely, because strict definitions were frequently omitted by the legislature deliberately, in order to enable our qualified judges to place their own interpretations on expressions such as these. It is planned to retain homosexuality as grounds for divorce, even if the Criminal Code is changed to the extent of not providing punishment for private homosexual acts between consenting adults.

BIGAMY

Another divorce offence is committed when one of the parties to the marriage "goes through a form of marriage with another person." It will be noted that no mention is made of the new union having adultery as a consequence. It is probably thought that the marriage has been desecrated to an extent sufficient to warrant its being dissolved, merely by the act of one party entering into a new "marriage". Nor, apparently, need the new "marriage" be performed with any particular ceremony. Any form, pretending to be a marriage, constitutes bigamy for the purposes of the Act.

CRUELTY

The third ground is possibly the most important one of the new divorce offences. It consists of the respondent party to the marriage "treating the petitioner with physical or mental cruelty of such a kind as to render intolerable the continued cohabitation of the spouses." The wording of the Act obviously prohibits a person from instituting divorce proceedings on the grounds of his own cruelty to his marriage partner.

Again, the Act gives a very general definition of cruelty. It can be left to the good sense of our judges to determine whether certain actions constitute cruelty for the purposes of granting a divorce or not. One English judge stated that he found difficulty in defining "cruelty", but that he found no difficulty in recognizing it where it existed.

Precedents. To aid in its decisions, the court can lean on numerous modern cases involving cruelty in related jurisdictions, particularly in England where cruelty has been grounds for divorce since 1937 and where (according to a Canadian case of 1955) the law of cruelty is held to be the same as in Canada. While not previously grounds for divorce in Canada (except in Nova Scotia), cruelty has been of legal significance here in the following connections:

- Cruelty is grounds for judicial separation in many of our provinces.
- Before 1925, a woman suing for divorce had to rely on her husband's cruelty as additional grounds for divorce in many cases.
- Until the 1968 Act, the petitioner's cruelty could be a conducing factor to the respondent's adultery and a *discretionary bar* to the divorce. (*See* page 90.)

The decisions of a Superior Court in all these cases constitute precedents for the guidance of the courts in cases covered by the new Act.

To serve as divorce grounds, cruelty must clearly encompass more than the ordinary wear and tear of married life. It must consist of grave and weighty conduct, which is not of accidental origin and which endangers the other party's life, limb, or health, be it physical or mental. As long as the act is intentional, no intent to injure need accompany it. To obtain relief, the victim, generally, had to have reasonable grounds for apprehending a repetition of the act of cruelty. However, the Alberta and Saskatchewan statutes dealing with judicial separation define cruelty to include any course of conduct which is so grossly insulting and intolerable that no reasonable person could be expected to continue living with a person who had been guilty of such conduct. The wording of the new Act is obviously very similar to this.

Exceptions. Even severe cruelty is not grounds for divorce when the petitioner consented to it of his own free will. Nor can a petitioner avail himself of the cruelty grounds when he provoked the cruelty by his own conduct, for example, nagging by a wife or hectoring by a husband to such an intense degree that a reasonable person would be deprived of his self-control.

The pleaded cruelty must amount to substantially more than burning the toast or eating crackers in bed; but nagging, reproaches and accusations, provided they are persistent and injurious to the other's health, are certainly valid grounds to substantiate cruelty.

In the following English situations, divorces were granted on the grounds of cruelty:

- A man's brutality to his child.
- A man's cruelty to his child in front of his wife.
- A man forcing his wife to prostitute herself.
- Prolonged refusal of intercourse.
- Grossly excessive or revolting sexual demands.
- The use of contraceptives or coitus interruptus against the other spouse's wishes.
- Communicating venereal disease to one's spouse.
- A man insisting on intercourse with his wife, when both knew him to have venereal disease.
- A hypochondriac wife unreasonably robbing her husband of sleep.
- Refusal to cooperate over important family matters.
- A man consistently flaunting his association with other women; whether actually existing or vindictively invented.
- Persistent and groundless accusations of adultery.
- Extreme personal uncleanliness.
- A wife's mania for cleaning the house, amounting to an obsession.
- A criminal conviction resulting in injury to the petitioner's health, for example, for indecent exposure.
- Systematic neglect and insults.
- Prolonged periods of taciturnity or sulkiness.
- Frequent abusive, intemperate and obscene language to one's wife in front of other people.

Drunkenness and gambling, by themselves, are not cruelty unless pursued to such a degree that they become a danger to the other's health.

Although wilful nonsupport of his wife and children by a man has been held to be an act of cruelty in England, it has not been included as specific grounds for divorce in the new Act.

Evidence. In undefended divorce cases, the court will usually require some impartial corroborative evidence of the act of cruelty which has been alleged by the petitioner. Examples would be bruises or complaints voiced by the victim at, or immediately after, the act of cruelty.

INSANITY AND ILLNESS

Incurable insanity and protracted illness have not, as such, been made grounds for divorce by the new Act. If the other spouse wishes to have the marriage dissolved on those grounds, he can avail himself of the provisions in another section of the Act, namely three years' separation. (*See* page 83.)

MARRIAGE BREAKDOWN

In addition to these new matrimonial offences, the 1968 Act provides for divorce on the grounds of a permanent breakdown of the marriage due to:

- The respondent's imprisonment for three (sometimes two) years.
- The respondent's addiction to alcohol or drugs.
- The respondent's disappearance for three years.
- Non-consummation of the marriage for one year.
- Separation of the parties for three years.
- Desertion by either party for five years.

These acts do not, of themselves, actually terminate a marriage. They merely form the basis for a divorce petition if they were the actual cause of a marriage breaking down permanently, and only if the husband and wife are living separate and apart and are not likely to resume cohabitation.

Imprisonment. A permanent breakdown of the marriage is deemed to have occurred if the previously described circumstances exist and if the respondent has spent three years, or more, in prison after having been convicted for one or more offences. The imprisonment may consist of one uninterrupted term or several terms, if they total at least three years in the five-year period immediately preceding the petition.

The petition can be presented after the respondent has been imprisoned for just two years, provided this period was part of a commuted death sentence or a ten-year sentence or more, and provided the respondent has exhausted all his rights to appeal. These periods refer to time actually spent in prison and not to any time spent out on parole, or for other grounds. The Act does not specify imprisonment in Canada, so that legal imprisonment anywhere else is also covered, but probably not kidnapping by individual or government gangsters.

While, in theory, a person's persistent and habitual criminality might be commendable grounds for divorcing him, it was felt that they were not sufficient grounds for practical purposes. Actual imprisonment is something easily capable of proof and it should be a satisfactory substitute for criminality.

Alcohol and Drug Addiction. The new Act also assumes a marriage breakdown exists after the respondent has, for at least three years immediately preceding the petition, been grossly addicted to alcohol or to a narcotic, without reasonable expectation of rehabilitation within a reasonably foreseeable period. The cause of the addiction is of no immediate consequence; thus, it makes no difference if the respondent was driven to the addiction by his spouse.

The *Narcotic Control Act* defines a person as being addicted to narcotics if "through the use of narcotics, he has developed a desire or need to continue their use, or if he has developed a psychological or physical dependence on their effects."

The term "grossly" is not defined further in the Act. The court will probably be guided by the opinion of medical observers in this regard. Evidence of unsuccessful attempts at a cure will probably contradict *reasonable* expectations of rehabilitation within a *reasonable* time. The court will, doubtless, also take account of the respondent's previous convictions for offences involving the use of narcotics and alcohol.

In divorce petitions based on addiction, it is no bar to the proceedings that the parties lived together during part, or all, of the three-year period, provided the petitioner is no longer living with the respondent at the time of applying for the divorce.

Disappearance. We have seen that it is possible to have a spouse presumed legally dead after an absence of seven years, so that it is permissible for the other party to marry again, without the fear of committing bigamy. (*See* page 6.) There is still the danger, however, of the first spouse "returning from the dead" with the result that the second marriage would be void and any children resulting from it could be, technically, illegitimate in some provinces.

This situation is cured by the new Act, which allows the petitioner to apply for a divorce if, for three years immediately prior to the application, he has had no knowledge or information as to the other's whereabouts and has been unable to locate him throughout that period. This wording of the Act, presumably, still requires the petitioner to make the same *reasonable efforts* to locate the respondent as the Ontario Marriage Act specifically requires of him.

A divorce on these grounds, as on any other, dissolves the marriage and leaves the couple free to enter new marriages, without the possible danger of bastardizing the children of the subsequent marriage(s) in some provinces.

Service of Papers. Normally, the court insists on elaborate safeguards to ensure that all papers in an action have been properly served on the other party. Seldom are these relaxed by an *order for substituted service* (for example by a registered letter to his last-known address), not even in a case during the last war, when the respondent was an enemy alien. However, a case of disappearance obviously calls for a relaxation of this rule. Divorce papers can now be served in any province of Canada, regardless in which province they were issued, and anywhere in the United States of America, without special leave of the court. (*See* page 94.)

Non-consummation. We have seen that impotence, or inability to consummate a marriage, was grounds for having the marriage annulled. (*See* page 49.) The new Act makes it grounds for divorce if the marriage has remained unconsummated for at least one year not only because of the respondent's disability, but also because of his illness (physical or psychological) or his refusal to consummate the marriage.

This provision will release couples who married "in name only" from their marriage ties. For example, people may marry to circumvent the immigration laws, to give the baby a name, for purely financial or economic reasons, to make the one party ineligible to give evidence against the other in a criminal trial, or to escape being sued in tort by the other party, on the principle "if you can't fight them, join them."

Proven impotence still serves to render a marriage null, without the one-year waiting period. Refusal, or inability to continue sexual intercourse is not grounds for divorce by itself. The former might constitute cruelty, however; and either may cause the three-year separation, discussed next.

Separation and Desertion. Possibly, the most frequent basis of divorce petitions, henceforth, will be the provision of the Act which permits divorce after the parties have been living separate and apart for a continuous period of at least three years, with no likelihood of cohabitation ever being resumed. The Act requires no reason to be stated for the separation. It can come about through disinterest, incompatibility, mutual consent, physical or mental illness, or by desertion. In a case of desertion, however, if it is the deserting party who is seeking the divorce, the separation must have lasted for five years before he is allowed to present his petition.

If it is in dispute whether an absence constitutes desertion, the same rules will be used to establish this as in England, where desertion is grounds for divorce, and as in those provinces which grant a judicial separation on the basis of desertion. (*See* page 34.) Canada may well be the first country to allow a party to come to the court for relief on the basis of his own wrongdoing, namely his desertion.

It will also have been noted that a three-year separation due to sickness or insanity is sufficient grounds for a marriage breakdown to be claimed by either spouse, if so desired, regardless of any marriage vows made concerning "in sickness or in health."

Exceptions. The court will refuse to grant a divorce on the basis of separation or desertion, if the granting of the decree would be "unduly harsh or unjust to either spouse; or if it would prejudicially affect the making of reasonable arrangements for the maintenance of either spouse." It is this provision which will restrain unscrupulous deserters from tossing off their responsibilities wantonly.

To encourage reconciliations, the Act allows separated parties to resume cohabitation in an attempt to achieve that purpose, without this cohabitation counting as an interruption of the three-or five-year separation periods. However, for this period of cohabitation not to count as condonation, there may be no more than one such interruption of the separation period, and it must last no longer than ninety days. (*See* page 67.) It will be remembered that the same ninety-day period of attempted reconciliation is not regarded as a condonation of adultery; nor does it condone the other, newly-created matrimonial offences of cruelty, etc.

Children. The court will not grant a divorce on any of the foregoing five marriage breakdown grounds if there are children of the marriage, and if a divorce would "prejudicially affect the making of reasonable arrangements for their maintenance." And, in repetition, the court will not grant a divorce in these five instances if there is a reasonable expectation that cohabitation will occur, or recur, within a reasonably foreseeable period.

MUTUAL CONSENT

As was seen earlier, separation by mutual consent now constitutes valid divorce grounds, provided all the concomitant requirements are also met. As a matter of fact, many separated parties draw up separation agreements to regulate such matters between them as finances, and the custody and care of the children. (*See* page 32 and Appendix.) It is naturally wisest for a lawyer to draft a document of such importance. The existence of a separation agreement assumes the absence of desertion. But, while the parties may separate by consent, it is not their prerogative to dissolve the marriage by consent. A dissolution can be achieved only by a judge, after a court trial.

chapter 8

THE NEW DIVORCE LAWS: OTHER IMPORTANT INNOVATIONS

RECONCILIATION

Except where it is obviously inappropriate (for example, the disappearance of one spouse), the new Act requires the lawyers for both parties to discuss the possibility of reconciliation with their clients, to advise them of the contents of the Act in this regard, and to inform them of any available counselling or guidance facilities. The Act now makes a legal requirement of a course of conduct which all ethical lawyers have consistently followed in the past. The Act requires the petitioner's lawyer to sign a statement on the petition to the effect that he has complied with these requirements of the Act.

While not specifically so stated in the Act, the requirement regarding reconciliation attempts probably applies only to cases involving marriage breakdown, and not to the so-called marital offence cases. It is interesting to note that an estimated 33% of the unhappily married couples coming before the Conciliation Courts of California, are said to be reunited.

As double assurance that nothing regarding a possible reconciliation has been overlooked, the Act imposes a duty on the divorce judge to precede the hearing of the evidence in the case, by questions to the petitioner (and to the respondent, if he is present in court) concerning the possibility of a reconciliation.

Academically, this requirement is an interesting innovation in our legal procedure. It requires a judge to act *inquisitorially*, that is, to become involved in the trial personally, in the manner of a European Interrogating Justice. This method is in contrast to our traditional *adversary method,* wherein the judge merely listens impartially to the arguments presented to him by the parties to the action, while maintaining proper court procedure, and then generally renders his decision on the basis of the presented arguments alone.

If in this questioning, or at any later time in the proceedings, the judge feels that there exists a possibility of reconciliation, he must adjourn the case and nominate a suitable person (a trained marriage counsellor preferably or perhaps a church minister) to try to assist the parties toward a reconciliation. If these efforts are unsuccessful, and fourteen days have elapsed after the adjournment, either party may apply to have the proceedings resumed.

Any communications made to this counsellor are *privileged,* which means, that they are not admissible as evidence in any legal proceedings.

It is sincerely hoped that the above provisions will do more than render lip service to an ideal, and will prove to be of genuine benefit to many people.

COURTS

The new Act specifies that divorce hearings shall be conducted in the Superior Court, or any of its branches, of all the provinces and Territories, with the temporary exception of Quebec and Newfoundland. (*See* page 89.)

This provision is contrary to the recommendation of the Joint Committee, which would have preferred divorce jurisdiction to be placed in the hands of the lower-ranking County and District Courts. This provision was also strongly attacked during the passage of the bill through Parliament, on the grounds that divorce cases could be handled more expeditiously, and at less cost, in the lower courts. It was estimated that it would cost $200-300 to try a divorce case in the County Court, as against $600-800 in the Superior Courts.

It was also claimed that the personal touch would be lacking in divorce cases which were heard at *Assizes,* a periodic court session, by a Superior Court judge on circuit. If a hearing was adjourned for an attempted reconciliation or, if a maintenance order was violated and required enforcement by the court, it would not likely be the same Superior Court judge, but a different one, who would hear the continuation of the case. On the other hand, if the local County Court judge had heard the petition, he would be the one to hear its continuation also, and thus be fully cognizant of the background of the case.

One of the chief reasons for ignoring these arguments was that, in view of the complications already caused by the new laws coming into effect, it should not be attempted to achieve too much all at once; and that a change in the system of jurisdiction would be premature. More uniformity in the interpretation of the new laws would also be attained if their administration was left in the hands of the Superior Court judges. Furthermore, should there be an insufficient number of Superior Court judges available to handle the increased number of divorce cases which were anticipated as a result of the new Act, it is open to each province to pass legislation which would permit County Court judges to act as Superior Court judges for certain periods or purposes. Ontario and British Columbia already possess such legislation.

One member of the Senate, with tongue in cheek perhaps, wondered if there would be enough lawyers available to handle all the increased business. A frequently quoted estimate is an initial doubling of the present rate of 10-11,000 divorces per year in Canada. Actually, 1,120 divorce petitions were filed in Toronto from July 2 to August 28, 1968. This represents about 28 divorce petitions per business day, as contrasted to about 18 per day previously. (The average total of all other civil claims lodged daily in the Toronto High Court offices at Osgoode Hall is 22.) In Quebec, 963 divorce applications were lodged during the same period; this is in contrast to 670 Quebec divorces in the Senate during all of 1967. On the basis of experience in other countries, it is expected that the liberalization of the divorce laws will result in divorce petitions levelling off to a 50% increase over the former figures.

The following breakdown gives the grounds on which divorce petitions were based from July 2 to August 24.

Separation	569
Adultery	154
Desertion (petition by deserter)	141
Cruelty (physical)	97
" (mental)	38
Alcoholism	11
Non-consummation (refusal)	6
Non-consummation (illness)	2

Disappearance	4
Bigamy	3
Imprisonment	2
Sodomy	2
TOTAL	1029

Some divorce cases based on the new laws are scheduled for hearing at the end of October 1968, even ahead of cases begun before July 2, 1968.

On the same occasion Senator Jean-François Pouliot repeated the prophetic speculation of Gordon Fairweather, M.P., that the Minister of Justice would probably become Prime Minister of Canada eventually, as a result of this piece of legislation.

Nova Scotia

Heretofore, a Nova Scotia law permitted divorce cases to be tried by County Court judges. On the face of it, the federal statute takes this power away from them; thus, apparently halving the number of judges available to try divorce cases in Nova Scotia. It was pointed out, however, that there is nothing to prevent the County Court judges from being appointed *pro tem* members of the Supreme Court.

New Brunswick

As a consequence of the new Act, it will no longer be necessary to have all New Brunswick divorce cases heard in Fredericton, the capital, as heretofore. They can now be heard at any other sitting of the Supreme Court in the province.

Quebec and Newfoundland

Since the courts of Quebec and Newfoundland did not have the power to grant divorces, residents could not get a divorce in their own courts. (The situation was similar in Ontario until 1930.) Until the passing of the new Act, Parliament performed this service for them, at a total cost of approximately $1000-1500 more than the cost of a provincial divorce including Parliament's fee of $120. It is interesting that in spite of the new legislation, Parliament still retains the right, constitutionally, to pass a private bill for the divorce of anyone, whether residing inside Canada or out of it. This is a good illustration of Parliament's retention of power.

EXCHEQUER COURT

In 1963, the cumbersome Parliamentary divorce machinery was greatly improved by making Newfoundland and Quebec divorces a matter to be decided by the Senate alone. Under the new Act, a Divorce Division of the Exchequer Court was created to hear these cases. It will also hear divorce cases where the parties live in different provinces and hence a deadlock arises as to the province in which the case should be tried. (*See* page 91.) The judges of this new Divorce Division will travel to all parts of Canada, so that it will no longer be necessary for the involved parties to make time-consuming and expensive trips to Ottawa from distant points.

Persons from Quebec and Newfoundland who have already lodged petitions to the Senate before the passing of the Act, can either allow their cases to continue there, or they may withdraw them at little cost, in order to take advantage of the streamlined new procedure.

Appeals from the decisions of this newly created Divorce Division must be made to the Exchequer Court, where three judges must hear the divorce appeals.

Whenever the provincial governments of Newfoundland and Quebec decide to try divorce cases in their own courts, the new Act makes provision for an immediate transfer of jurisdiction, by an Order in Council, from the Divorce Division of the Exchequer Court to the respective Superior Courts of the two provinces. Quebec and Newfoundland took this step in September of 1968.

TRIALS

From now on, divorce hearings will always be conducted by a judge alone, without a jury. The trial is generally open to the public, but in some provinces (Ontario for example) the judge has the right to exclude the public if he wishes.

The evidence on which the judge grants the decree must consist of something beyond the "consent, admissions, or default of the parties, or either of them". This requirement will probably entail a change in the procedure of the Alberta courts which, in many cases, required no corroboration of a respondent's admission of having committed adultery.

DISCRETIONARY BARS

It can be taken for granted that almost all the *discretionary bars* to divorce have been repealed. The section of the new Act which deals with bars to divorce is so specific that those which have not been expressly named in it, need not be presumed to survive.

We have already discussed *collusion*, which remains an absolute bar. We have also discussed *condonation* and *connivance*, which can now be regarded as the only surviving discretionary bars. For the sake of completeness, the following are the extinct bars:

- Undue Delay in starting divorce proceedings. This was abolished because the law makers probably felt that, if the delay is substantial, it will in all likelihood entail a separation of more than three years; which is grounds for divorce, in itself, today. The removal of this bar should have the beneficial effect of retaining the possibility of a reconciliation by not panicking a petitioner into premature legal proceedings for fear that he might become guilty of an undue delay.
- The petitioner's conduct conducing to the respondent's adultery, or other marital offence. This conduct could be the petitioner's cruelty, desertion, or neglect; under the new philosophy, these acts just serve to emphasize the breakdown of the marriage and will not deprive the petitioner of a divorce.
- The petitioner had to confess any adultery of his own. On the same reasoning as above, this no longer has a bearing on the outcome of the case. However, by committing any of these acts listed under the last two headings, the petitioner will probably be granted less favourable corollary relief and he himself could, naturally, be sued for divorce by the other party.

JURISDICTION

Under the new legislation, a person (whether a man or a woman) who is *domiciled* anywhere in Canada, may start divorce proceedings in the courts of any province in which either the petitioner or the respondent has been *ordinarily resident* for the year immediately preceding the presentation of the petition, and been *actually* resident for at least ten months of that period. If the petitioner has his residence in

Ontario, the trial must take place in the county town of the county in which either he or his spouse ordinarily resides. If the petitioner is *domiciled* in Canada and does not reside in Ontario but the respondent does, and the petitioner wants the case tried in Ontario, it will be tried in the county town of the county in which the respondent ordinarily resides.

It is noteworthy that domicile (for divorce purposes) is no longer restricted to any particular province, but is Canada-wide. Further, a married woman no longer automatically carries the domicile of her husband, but she has one of her own, even if she is under twenty-one years of age. Again, this applies to divorces only, and not annulments.

A Central Divorce Registry has been established in Ottawa through which divorce petitions from all over Canada must be cleared. One of the main purposes of this office is to eliminate the possibility of a second action being initiated in a different locality, after one of the spouses has already filed a petition. With the aid of its computers, recourse may seldom be necessary to the Act, which provides precedence for the earlier filed petition, and which arranges for a hearing by the Divorce Division of the Exchequer Court of petitions which were filed simultaneously. Detailed regulations were issued in June 1968, prescribing the steps to be taken by court officers all over the country to keep the Central Registry supplied with up-to-date information.

Divorce decrees and orders for corollary relief which have been made in any province, have legal effect throughout Canada. (*See* page 97.) The latter can be enforced in any province, once the orders have been registered in the Superior Court of that province. The fee for such a registration in Ontario is $5.00.

This provision is similar to the ones contained in the Reciprocal Enforcement of Judgments and Maintenance Orders Acts of Ontario and other provinces.

chapter 9

COURT PROCEEDINGS

Earlier we saw that a couple cannot terminate their own marriage; it takes a court order to effect this, after a formal trial. A brief summary of the lawyers' activities in preparing for the trial is given here, followed by a description of the trial itself. It will be useful to learn the legal terms by which the parties to the divorce action are known. Also given will be the terms used in the various provinces until recently, since cases begun before the passing of the new legislation will continue to occupy the courts for some time.

LEGAL TERMINOLOGY

In Alberta, British Columbia, the Territories, Ontario, Prince Edward Island and Saskatchewan, the parties were termed the same as in other types of legal action. Thus, the person seeking the divorce or annulment was called the *plaintiff* and the other party was the *defendant*, the so-called *guilty party*. If the action was based on adultery, the person with whom the adultery was committed was also named as a defendant, generally called the *co-defendant* and sometimes (for example, in Alberta) the *co-adulterer*.

In Manitoba, New Brunswick, Nova Scotia, and in divorce proceedings before Parliament, the English terms are used: the person seeking the divorce is the *petitioner* and the other party is the *respondent*. The third party is generally called the *co-respondent*; in Manitoba, he is sometimes called the *co-adulterer* and in New Brunswick, he is the *co-adulterer* or *intervener*. The 1968 Divorce Act employs the terms *petitioner* and *respondent*, which should henceforth be used in all the provinces.

NECESSARY DOCUMENTS

The petitioner's lawyer begins the divorce or annulment proceedings by completing certain forms and having them approved and sealed by the Superior Court offices. (*See* Appendix.) The name for this document is now the *Petition* in all the provinces. This always was the name for it in England, Manitoba, New Brunswick, Nova Scotia, and in Parliament. In Ontario, the new rules of court require the petition to be accompanied by a document called the *Notice of Petition*. The petition sets out full particulars of the petitioner's claim:

- The names and addresses of all the parties;
- The nature of the remedy being sought, such as a divorce or an annulment;
- Details of the divorce or annulment grounds;
- Financial maintenance of the spouse and children;
- Custody of the children;
- The costs of the action.

Damages from the co-adulterer must now be sought in a separate action; but, with the court's permission, this second action may be tried concurrently with the divorce action. (*See* page 69.)

In British Columbia, Ontario, Prince Edward Island, Saskatchewan and the Yukon, a *Writ of Summons* had to be issued which contained the names of the parties to the action and the principal remedy sought (for example, divorce, separation, or annulment). This had to be accompanied by a *Statement of Claim* which detailed the balance of the above particulars. In Alberta and the NWT, the Statement of Claim was the only document that was required.

The petition must name the person with whom the adultery is alleged, if his name is known. It has been discussed earlier that every attempt must be made to establish his name; but, if this is not possible, the court will, upon request, grant leave for his name to be omitted. (*See* page 65.) However, if the petitioner claims to be ignorant of the third party's name, and it is then shown that he really did know the name, his petition will be dismissed. If the divorce is sought on the basis of the respondent's conviction for the crime of rape, sodomy, or bigamy, the victim of the offence need not be made a respondent, unless a judge otherwise orders.

SERVICE OF DOCUMENTS

The next step is to *serve* the documents on the respondents. In Ontario, this must be done within 60 days after the issue of the documents. *Service* is best effected by a sheriff's officer or other official process server, although it is open to other people to serve the papers also. However, the petitioner or his lawyer may not do this; although the petitioner frequently accompanies the process server to help identify the respondent. The parties involved usually must be served personally with all documents in marriage dissolution cases, even if one is an enemy alien. Only if the court grants an *order for substituted service*, will it be permitted to mail the documents, or to leave them with someone other than the respondent, or to publish their contents in a series of newspaper advertisements as stipulated by the court. (*See* page 82.)

The process server then places on official record the place and the time of service, and the manner in which he was able to identify the person(s) served; (for example, from a photograph with which he had been previously furnished). Usually, he also obtains the served parties' signed acknowledgment of the service, which he then witnesses with his own signature. The purpose of all these precautionary measures is to make absolutely sure that no one accidentally gets divorced without his knowledge.

PLEADINGS

If the respondent wants to defend the case, he must *make an answer* to the petition, or *enter an appearance* within a specified number of days (ranging from 8 to 40 days in the different provinces) and, sometimes, lodge a *defence* or *answer* or *response* within a short period of time after that. The italicized words are the names of documents which the respondent's lawyer fills out on the basis of his client's instructions and which he deposits in court and serves on the petitioner. After this, there may be still further *pleadings,* such as:

- A *reply* by the petitioner to the respondent's *answer*;
- A *counter-petition* by the respondent;
- And an *answer* by the petitioner to the respondent's *counter-petition.*

There are many other intermediate steps which frequently must be taken before the case comes up for trial, such as a request for the court to order:

- Interim alimony to the wife;
- Suit money in the Maritimes;
- Temporary care, custody and upbringing of the children;
- Relief from the obligation to cohabit with the other spouse.

THE TRIAL

Undefended Actions. If the action is undefended, for example, if the respondent fails to file an answer, all that is required is to give formal evidence of the facts stated in the petition (or, previously, in the Statement of Claim). It must be shown that:

- The proceedings were brought in the proper court.
- All the involved parties were properly served with the relevant documents. Then:
- The circumstances upon which the divorce petition is based (adultery, etc.) must be satisfactorily proved.
- The court must be satisfied as to the absence of collusion, connivance, and condonation.
- It must be shown that all the necessary steps have been taken to try to achieve a reconciliation.

Defended Actions. If the action is defended, the respondent may deny the commission of the matrimonial offence which has been alleged, or the existence of a marriage breakdown. He can do this by calling his own witnesses, and by attacking the credibility of the petitioner and his witnesses in cross-examination. It may be that the divorce itself is not contested, but that the respondent disagrees with the petitioner's demands for a financial settlement and his demands to be awarded custody of the children, etc.

JUDGMENT

At the conclusion of the trial, the judge may decide to refuse to grant the divorce or annulment. But if he does grant it, it will be in the form of a *decree nisi.* (*See* page 52 for exceptions.) This is a conditional decree which will be made *absolute* or final, provided the decision is not successfully appealed to a court of appeal, and provided no material facts come to light which could result in the decree being rescinded, (such as a reconciliation or evidence of collusion). While any person may bring such facts to the attention of the court, it is often the Queen's Proctor who uncovers collusion, etc., either of his own initiative or at the instigation of the judge who conducted the trial. (*See* page 64.)

Since the Divorce Act of 1968 is not concerned with annulments, it does not change the different rules of the provinces regarding the issue of a *decree absolute* of annulment. But a decree absolute of dissolution henceforth, can be applied for three months after the issue of the *decree nisi* in all the provinces. In Manitoba, Ontario and Prince Edward Island, the rules of court required that the petitioner swear in his application for a *decree absolute* that he has not lived or cohabited with the respondent since the date of the granting of the *decree nisi.* The new Ontario rules require the petitioner's lawyer to certify that he has not been served with an appeal from the decree nisi, or with a notice that someone plans to show cause against the decree nisi being made absolute. The three-month period can be shortened, or even eliminated, if in the opinion of the judge, it is in the public interest to adopt this procedure and if the parties undertake not to appeal the decision.

APPEALS

An appeal against the decision in a divorce trial can be lodged within fifteen days of the granting of the *decree nisi.* On special grounds, a judge of the appeal court may grant an extension of this period. The decision of the appeal court may be appealed on a point of law to the Supreme Court of Canada within 30 days, or more sometimes, with leave of that court. Provided there has been no appeal from the granting of the *decree nisi,* and the petitioner has made no application to have the decree made absolute after the three-month period, the respondent then has the right to make such an application four months after the *decree nisi.* The court then has the power to make the decree absolute if there exist no circumstances to prohibit it, such as the previously mentioned reconciliation or collusion.

Once a divorce has been made absolute, it is too late to appeal it, and the divorced parties are at immediate liberty to remarry. But an absolute decree of annulment can be appealed in some provinces (for example, Ontario), if a party can show that he had no opportunity to appeal the *decree nisi,* in which case the right to remarry is delayed until the appeal has been heard.

COROLLARY OR ANCILLARY RELIEF

Almost as important as the dissolution of the marriage itself, are the provisions which are made by the court regarding the couple's finances and the future of any children of the marriage. Very similar dispositions are made in judicial separations.

Children. Pending the hearing and determination of the divorce petition, the court has the power to make any *interim,* that is, provisional, order it thinks fit and just, for the financial maintenance and the custody, care and upbringing of the children of the marriage who are under the age of sixteen years; or over sixteen, but unable to provide for themselves due to illness, disability, etc.

If there exist any such children, the Ontario rules of court require a copy of the divorce petition to be served on the *Official Guardian* of the province. This officer conducts an inquiry regarding the needs and interests of the children, usually through the Children's Aid Societies, and then makes his report on them to the court in official evidence.

Custody. When the *decree nisi* is granted, the court will make a final order regarding these children, subject, however, to the court's power to vary its order subsequently. (*See* page 100.) At common law, the father was the parent with the primary right to the children's custody, regardless of his conduct and morals. Today, the children's best interests are the principal determining factor in the court's decision in this regard. The term *custody* technically means overall responsibility; while *care* means the physical charge of the child. When divorces were granted solely on the basis of a matrimonial offence having been committed, *custody* was usually given to the *innocent* party rather than to the *guilty* party. This distinction has become academic since the recent introduction of divorces based on a marriage breakdown, which can come about through no fault of any one person in particular.

Therefore, it is only the best interests of the child which will determine into which parent's custody he shall be placed. In some cases, children are ordered to be placed in the care of grandparents, etc. A child of tender years is, normally, best left with its mother. This is the order most frequently made, even when she was found guilty of adultery, provided the tone in her household is not of such an immoral nature as to have a harmful effect on the child. Brothers and sisters are usually not separated, but left with the same parent whenever possible and advisable.

Access. Unless it is considered definitely harmful to the child, the other parent is usually given liberal, but rigidly prescribed *rights of access,* ranging from periodic short visits, to taking the child away for a few hours at a time, for some weekends, or even for a month's holiday. This right of access may even be given a parent who is living "common law", provided the tone in his home is not otherwise immoral.

Parties to a divorce frequently draft an agreement regarding finances and the care of the children. If the court finds no objection to the terms of this agreement, it can approve it.

If neither party to the action makes any claims regarding the children, the court will, on its own initiative, investigate the circumstances and make such orders regarding the children as it deems proper.

Removal from the Jurisdiction. It is a customary term of the court's custody order to prohibit the child from being taken *out of the jurisdiction* (which means outside the province) without the leave of the court. A violation of this prohibition constitutes a contempt of court and can be subject to punishment; particularly, if the child's interests, or the other parent's rights are harmed thereby.

If there is no such prohibition in the order, the child may be taken outside the jurisdiction for purposes which are not unreasonable. The reason for these provisions is the fact that the court loses the power to supervise the child's welfare once the child is outside the court's jurisdiction.

Alimony and Maintenance. The term *alimony* is loosely used by the public for any payments which a husband makes to his separated or divorced wife. Strictly speaking, *alimony* should be reserved for payments to a separated spouse; while the payments made to a former spouse should properly be called *maintenance.*

The Divorce Act of 1968 has made very sweeping provisions regarding the payment of alimony and maintenance for the parties to a divorce. The Act makes no provision for the parties to separation or annulment proceedings, so that the previously existing provincial rules regarding these matters remain unchanged.

As a result of the new Act, women have achieved full equality with men in one regard: payments are no longer automatically made by the man to the woman, but are to be made by the spouse who has the means, to the spouse who is in need.

Interim Orders. After the presentation of the divorce petition, the court will usually make an interim order relieving the parties from their obligation to cohabit with one another. The court will also make any order it thinks fit and just, for the payment of *alimony* (or an *alimentary pension*) by either spouse for the maintenance of the other spouse until the divorce case is terminated. The alimony is designed to maintain the needy spouse reasonably, but at little more than a subsistence level. It is also based on the financial means and needs of both persons. To help the court assess the means of each person, the petition and the answer will have outlined particulars of the couple's means, and the court has the power to order an examination of the couple in this regard.

Final Orders. After the granting of the *decree nisi,* the court will take into consideration the means, condition, and other circumstances of both the parties. It will also consider the conduct of the couple and order either the husband or the wife to secure, or to pay, either a lump sum or periodic sums, which the court thinks reasonable, for the maintenance of the other spouse and/or for the maintenance of the children of the marriage.

When determining the amount of an order for maintenance or permanent alimony for an innocent spouse, the court takes into account the standard of life which the couple can afford and fixes an amount which is in keeping with it. A fund can be ordered established for the children out of the funds of either, or both the spouses.

The court has the power to attach any such terms, conditions or restrictions to the order as it pleases. For example, the court may delay granting the *decree absolute* until any trust deed it has ordered to be drawn up has been properly executed. The court can order the payments to be made either to the spouse directly, or to a trustee or administrator on his behalf.

A sum is said to be *secured* to the other spouse if it is placed into the hands of a trustee with irrevocable instructions to make payment(s) to the spouse according to the instructions contained in the deed of trust. If the security should lose its value, that is the beneficiary's misfortune.

Agreements. The court must make decisions in the foregoing matters if the couple is in dispute regarding them. However, as mentioned earlier, the couple frequently comes to an agreement, even in defended cases, regarding monetary matters and the future of the children. In such cases, the draft agreement must be submitted to the court, and the agreement will not become effective until the court approves its terms. It should be noted that any clause in such an agreement whereby one of the parties waives his right to seek relief from the court when needed, is ineffective.

Variation of Orders. The court has the power to vary its order subsequently with regard to any of the above matters, or even to rescind it, if it thinks fit and just to do so in view of the intervening conduct of the parties, or if there has been any change in the condition, means, or other circumstances of either party. The court also has the power to vary the terms of any marriage settlement which existed for the benefit of the couple and their children, so as to make proper allowance for the changed circumstances occasioned by the divorce.

As mentioned earlier, the power of the court to vary its order also extends to any orders it made regarding the welfare of the children.

The federal Act does not empower the divorce court to order *separate maintenance,* that is to arrange for a division of the family property between the divorced couple.

ANNULMENTS

In annulment cases, as was explained earlier, reference still has to be made to the previously existing provincial laws. Since they are all based on the old English laws, the various provincial laws are very similar. The following is a summary of the Ontario Matrimonial Causes Act, 1960; the laws of the other provinces are referred to only in cases of difference.

The Ontario Act authorizes the court to order the husband to secure to the wife (but not *vice versa*) a gross or annual sum of money not to exceed her lifetime, which sum it deems reasonable, based on the wife's fortune, the husband's financial ability, and the conduct of the parties.

Additionally, or instead, the court may order the husband to make periodic unsecured payments to his wife of such amounts as the court thinks reasonable. The court may subsequently order an increase or decrease of the payments, discharge the order, suspend it, or revive it. Unless discharged earlier, such an order ceases when either of the spouses dies, or if the wife remarries.

Alimony. Alimony payments cannot be ordered to be secured, but a judgment for alimony can be charged against any land the husband owns, in the same manner as other court judgments.

If alimony is sought, independently of any request for a dissolution of the marriage, it is not necessary to apply for it to the Superior Court. It can also be obtained in the lower-ranking Family Courts or Division Courts (small claims courts). (*See* page 40.)

A person making alimony payments pursuant to a court order or after entering a written separation agreement is entitled to deduct them from his income for income tax purposes. On the other hand, alimony payments must be shown as taxable income by the recipient.

The Ontario Act dealt with both divorces and annulments but the federal Divorce Act of 1968 enacted a general repeal of all provincial legislation involving divorce. Consequently, mention of certain provisions of the Ontario Act has been deliberately omitted, as obviously referring to divorces only; for example, the *chastity* (*dum casta*) *clause,* which ended payments to a wife who committed adultery or who did not remain chaste.

In Manitoba, a claim for maintenance cannot be joined with a petition for annulment, but must be lodged in a separate action.

In Alberta, the court may issue an injunction to prevent the husband from disposing of his property in a manner to defeat an alimony order which has been made, or is about to be made, against him.

INFANTS

If the petitioner in a matrimonial cause is a *minor* or an *infant,* that is under twenty-one years of age, he must institute proceedings through a person called his *next friend,* who virtually guarantees that the infant will obey any court orders made against him and pay all the court costs for which he might be made responsible.

If the infant is a respondent to the action, he must be represented by a *guardian at law* (guardian *ad litem*) who can be appointed for him by the court or who can be the Official Guardian.

Mentally Incompetent Persons. These people have to be represented in court actions by a *next friend*, a guardian *ad litem*, or by an administrator called a *committee* (accented on the first syllable). Any of these representatives is empowered to act on behalf of the mentally incompetent person, even to the extent of making sworn statements to the best of his belief, in documents (such as *affidavits*) which the incompetent person would normally have to do himself.

If the respondent is mentally incompetent, it is the petitioner's responsibility to have a guardian appointed for him by the court, who will receive service of all necessary documents on his behalf.

COSTS

The decision as to who is to bear the court costs in a law suit lies entirely in the discretion of the court. In a normal law suit, the loser is usually made to bear his own court costs and also to pay for many of those incurred by the winner. An exception is made in the case of a successful plaintiff who initiated action in a trivial matter purely for frivolous or vexatious purposes.

In a matrimonial case, the husband traditionally bears the entire court costs, whether he be winner or loser, guilty of immoral conduct, or innocent. This need not be the case however, if the wife's conduct and personal fortune incline the court to decide otherwise. A co-respondent may also be made to pay any additional costs which his unwarranted tactics may have occasioned.

In Ontario, the court fees for a straightforward divorce (from the petition to the decree absolute) are $70. It is estimated that a lawyer charges $600 for an undefended divorce case. Free Legal Aid is available, however, in certain cases.

chapter 10

THE DIVORCÉE (AND WIDOW) AND THE LAW

A decree absolute of divorce or an annulment on voidable grounds puts an end to a marriage; and, the annulment of a void "marriage" is a declaration that a marriage never existed between the couple. In both cases, the ex-spouses are free to live their separate lives thereafter; they may even marry again, subject to the waiting period for a possible appeal in some annulment cases. When Parliament grants a divorce, the Private Act specifically grants them the right to remarry.

AFTER EFFECTS

Name of Divorced Wife. A divorced woman can continue to use her husband's name or she can revert to her maiden name as she chooses. It makes no difference in this regard, as it does in some European countries, whether the wife was the innocent or guilty party to the divorce. Equally, a widow who remarries and then divorces her second husband, may choose to resume the use of her first husband's name. As a matter of fact, any person in Canada may use any name that he pleases, as long as he does not do so with the intention of defrauding anyone, or in violation of some specific statute. It is a simple matter to change one's name officially by complying with the requirements of the various provincial Change of Name Acts. If a divorced woman wishes, she may continue using the title which her divorced husband bears, even when she remarries.

Etiquette. On all formal correspondence, including visiting cards, a divorcée, but not a separated wife, replaces her husband's Christian name with her maiden name. As an example,

Mrs. George Smith, who was Mary Jones, should call herself Mrs. Jones Smith and not Mrs. Mary Smith.

Divorced parents should not issue a joint invitation to the wedding of their children. They should attend a family wedding with their new husbands and wives respectively.

It is socially incorrect to send out engraved invitations or announcements of the marriage of a divorcée; instead, handwritten notes should be mailed to close friends. The fact that the groom has been divorced does not prevent his bride from sending out marriage announcements or invitations.

It is considered poor taste for a divorcée to wear the white bridal dress and veil which are typical for a virginal bride. If she wishes to wear white, it should be a simple street-length dress, worn with a hat.

A widow usually wears her wedding ring until she dies or marries again. On the other hand, a divorcée may consider her wedding ring a symbol of failure and unhappiness and decide to discard it. Alternatively, she may wear it, or another ring of her own choosing on her right hand, to indicate that she has been married and might consider a second marriage.

Marital Status. Whether a woman is single, married, or a widow, can have serious legal consequences.

- We have already seen that an engagement ring, or other conditional gifts, may be kept by a divorced woman, but must be returned by a woman whose marriage was declared void *ab initio*. (*See* page 42.)
- Any gifts given by friends and relatives to the couple, or to either of them, "in contemplation of their forthcoming marriage" are returnable if the marriage does not take place, or if it is subsequently annulled. The gifts can be kept if the marriage takes place but ends in divorce. (As to which of the couple is entitled to keep the presents, *see* page 24.)
- A bequest in a will to a woman on condition "that she be unmarried" was held valid, even though the woman in question was divorced. Such a woman is a *feme sole*.
- In the case of a will which provided that a man was to receive the income from a fund for the rest of his life and that, after his death, the fund was to go to "his widow", his divorced wife was not entitled to benefit.
- The bequest of a life income by a man to "his widow" was cancelled when the marriage was subsequently declared void *ab initio*.

- If a man obtains a foreign divorce which is not regarded as valid in Canada, his wife retains any rights she had under her husband's insurance policy.
- A similar situation arose when a man, after obtaining a foreign divorce, married again and took out an insurance policy appointing "his wife" as his beneficiary. When his divorce was found to be invalid, the first wife benefited from the policy.

Dower. Any dower rights a wife may have in her husband's real property are extinguished after a divorce or annulment. (*See* page 28.) They remain subsisting after a separation, unless signed away by the wife or if she is guilty of uncondoned adultery. To quote the Ontario Dower Act of 1960 regarding *elopements*:

> "Where a wife willingly leaves her husband and goes away and continues with her adulterer, she is barred forever of her action to demand her dower that she ought to have of her husband's land, unless her husband willingly and without coercion is reconciled to her and suffers her to dwell with him, in which case she is restored to her action."

Insurance. Any rights a person has as a beneficiary under his spouse's insurance policy expire after a divorce or annulment, whether the spouse was specifically named in the policy by name or simply referred to as "my wife" or "my husband." An exception to this rule exists where the insured advised the insurance company that the beneficiary was to be *appointed irrevocably*. This is seldom done within the family but it is the procedure which is customarily adopted when the beneficiary has given the insured some *consideration* or value for taking out the policy in his favour.

In business, debtors are often induced to employ this procedure for the protection of their creditors while the debt remains unpaid. Partners frequently insure the lives of all their partners to enable them to buy out a deceased partner's share of the partnership from his estate under the "buy-sell" clause often contained in partnership agreements.

After a separation, a spouse does not cease to be a beneficiary, unless he is expressly removed as such from the policy by instructions to the insurance company. If he has been guilty of acts which are grounds for judicial separation in some of the provinces, his consent to his removal as a beneficiary is not required in any of the provinces, even though he is a *preferred beneficiary.* This was the name given to close relatives in policies until 1962.

If the beneficiary is *irrevocable,* he cannot be deprived of his benefits without his consent, whatever his marital status. If he agrees to give up his rights under the policy, he must send the insurance company his written consent to that effect. If he refuses to give his consent, the court may take this into account when determining the amount of corollary relief to be allotted on granting the divorce or separation. Allowance for the still-subsisting insurance rights will also be made in a separation agreement drawn up between the couple.

PENSIONS

Most pension plans which made provision for a pensioner's widowed spouse to continue receiving certain specified benefits after his death, do not extend such rights to a spouse who was divorced from the pensioner.

WILLS

Effect of Divorce, Etc. Any provision which has been made in a person's will for "my wife" or "my husband" is automatically revoked on divorce or annulment. A bequest by a Mr. Spouse to "my wife, Eve Spouse" will stand, because he may have continued on quite good terms with her, even after the divorce. Also, a bequest by a bachelor to "my wife" will stand in favour of a woman who can prove that she was generally considered to be his wife.

For a person to ensure that his *separated,* though not divorced, spouse shall not benefit from his will, a standard clause is generally placed in it stating that any benefits are conditional upon the spouse living with the testator at the time of his death.

Compulsory Provisions. Formerly a person could dispose of his fortune by his will in whatever manner he pleased. If he wanted to, a man could "cut off" his wife and children with the proverbial shilling and leave the balance of his fortune to his mistress or to the cats' home. This is still the case in Prince Edward Island and in Newfoundland.

The situation has been changed by statute in almost all English law jurisdictions, to conform with the principle existing in many European legal systems, whereby certain minimum amounts must be left to one's immediate family. The Quebec law in this regard has already been discussed. (*See* page 26.) In Saskatchewan, a widow must be left at least as much in her husband's will as she would have received on his intestacy. (*See* page 110.) The Ontario Dependants' Relief Act provides that the surviving dependent family members of the deceased are entitled to adequate amounts from his estate for their maintenance in accordance with the family's accustomed standards of life, if the will has not made provision for them adequately. Not falling within the category of persons entitled to such relief is the separated wife of a deceased man who, at the time of his death, was living in circumstances that would disentitle her to alimony.

DOWER

A widow's dower rights cannot be extinguished by any provision in the husband's will, unless the widow signed away her rights. (*See* page 28.) However, if the will contains a bequest to the widow which is conditional on her waiving her dower rights, she can accept the bequest on those conditions.

If the will mentions nothing regarding dower rights, a widow gets her dower rights in addition to whatever has been left to her in the will.

If the will makes certain provisions for a widow but attempts to take away her dower rights expressly, or by leaving to someone else the land which is subject to the dower, the widow can *elect* to take the dower rights in place of the other provisions made for her in the will.

Contesting a Will's Validity. Any person who feels that he was improperly omitted from the benefits of a will, may attack its validity in the provincial Probate or Surrogate Court on the grounds that the deceased was not of sound mind when he composed the will, or that he was acting under threats at the time, or that he otherwise failed to exercise his free will. This might be so if he was the victim of a fraud or if he was under the *undue influence* of some dominant person, such as his nurse, housekeeper, etc.

Beneficiaries as Witnesses. A person cannot receive any benefits under a will to which he, or his spouse, was a witness. Consequently, care should be taken not to witness the will of a friend or a relative, who might be expected to make a bequest to the solicited witness or his spouse.

Revocation of Wills. A will can be expressly revoked by its maker, the *testator,* in various ways and it is also automatically revoked when he marries or remarries. Consequently, if a person wishes his property to descend according to his will rather than according to the laws of intestacy, he should execute a new will immediately after getting married.

However, a will drawn up before marriage remains valid, if the testator states in it that it is drawn up "in contemplation of an impending marriage" to a specifically named person, and if his marriage to that particular person actually takes place.

Illegal Provisions. If a testator attaches any illegal conditions to a bequest, the beneficiary need not carry out the illegal condition and may benefit from the will regardless. The illegal condition need not involve the commission of a criminal act; for example, it is regarded by the law as contrary to public policy, and consequently illegal, to restrain unreasonably a person's freedom to marry. Therefore, if a will (or a contract, for that matter) attaches a condition which will prevent the beneficiary from getting married at all, or for an unreasonable length of time, or if it excludes from eligibility an unreasonably wide class of mates, then this restriction will be declared invalid by the court.

An example of a stipulation which was considered to be an unreasonable restraint of marriage, was contained in the will of a baptized Winnipeg Jew who left a large inheritance to his daughter on condition that she marry no one but a gentile.

On the other hand, a provision in the 1963 will of a Jewish testator in Port Perry, Ont. that his granddaughters were not to receive their inheritance until they had signed undertakings that they would lead strictly religious lives and marry only a man of their own faith, was held to be a not unreasonable, and therefore, an enforceable restraint of marriage.

It is not regarded as unreasonably restrictive for a man to provide for the termination of a life income to his widow when she remarries. Also valid is the bequest of an income to a girl until she gets married, if the bequest is obviously made to assist her until she finds a husband to provide for her. Then the condition is not interpreted as a marriage penalty.

INTESTACY

If a person dies *intestate,* without leaving a valid will or testament, provincial statutes govern the distribution of his estate. The deceased person's domicile usually decides which province's laws of wills and inheritance shall be applicable. (*See* page 52.)

The following chart shows the amounts which go to the surviving relatives. No intestacy benefits go to a spouse when a judicial separation has been ordered and the spouses have not resumed cohabitation. Where provision is made in the chart for a spouse to receive a specified lump sum of money he will receive the entire estate if it amounts to less than the lump sum.

PROVINCES	SURVIVORS	SPOUSE'S SHARE	BALANCE TO:
Alberta	Spouse & no child	Entire estate	——
	1 child	\$20,000 + ½ of balance	Child
	Children	\$20,000 + ⅓ of balance	Children
British Columbia	Spouse & no child	\$20,000 + ½ of balance	Deceased's kin
	1 child	½ of estate	Child
	Children	⅓ of estate	Children
Manitoba	Spouse & no child	Entire estate	——
	1 child	\$10,000 + ½ of balance	Child
	Children	\$10,000 + ⅓ of balance	Children
New Brunswick	Spouse & no child	Personal Chattels & \$50,000 + ½ of balance	Deceased's kin
	1 child	½ of estate	Child
	Children	⅓ of estate	Children
New-foundland	Spouse & no child	\$30,000 + ½ of balance	Deceased's kin
	1 child	½ of estate	Child
	Children	⅓ of estate	Children
NWT and Yukon	Spouse & no child	Entire estate	——
	1 child	½ of estate	Child
	Children	⅓ of estate	Children

PROVINCES	SURVIVORS	SPOUSE'S SHARE	BALANCE TO:
Nova Scotia	Spouse & no child	\$25,000 + ½ of balance	Deceased's kin
	1 child	\$25,000 + ½ of balance	Child
	Children	\$25,000 + ⅓ of balance	Children
Ontario	Widow & no child	\$20,000 & ⅔ of balance	Deceased's kin
	Widower & no child	½ of balance	Deceased's kin
	Widow & 1 child	½ of balance or Dower	Child
	Widower & 1 child	⅓ of balance or Curtesy	Child
	Spouse & children	⅓ of balance { or Dower / or Curtesy	Children
Prince Edward Island	Spouse & no child	\$8,000 + ½ of balance	Deceased's kin
	1 child	½ of estate	Child
	Children	⅓ of estate	Children
Quebec	Widow & no child	Community Property or ⅓ of estate	Deceased's kin
	Widower & no child	½ of estate	Deceased's kin
	Widow & 1 child	½ of estate	Child
	Widower & 1 child	⅓ of estate	Child
	Spouse & children	⅓ of estate	Children
Saskatchewan	Spouse & no child	Entire estate	——
	1 child	\$10,000 + ½ of balance	Child
	Children	\$10,000 + ⅓ of balance	Children

DEATH DUTIES

If a person feels impelled to leave a will for no other reason, a carefully drawn will serves a useful purpose in saving one's survivors substantial federal Estate Taxes and provincial Succession Duties. If the beneficiaries are the deceased's spouse and children, death duties are payable only on relatively large estates; but if the beneficiaries are not the deceased's closest relatives, they have to be paid on much smaller estates and at much higher rates.

It should not be overlooked that a survivor's estimated life income from the deceased person's pension and insurance, any copyright and patent royalties, etc., is capitalized on the basis of his normal life expectancy and is added to the value of the deceased person's estate for death duty purposes. The payment of provincial Succession Duty on such future income can be spread by a spouse over his estimated life expectancy, or ten years, whichever is less.

For example, the $200,000 estate of an Ontario man with two children under 21 would be saved about $3,300 in death duties if, instead of leaving his estate outright to his forty-five year old widow, he merely left her a life interest in his estate, with a provision for the capital to go to his children after her death. If there were three adult children and a sixty-year old widow, the duties on this estate would be reduced by about $26,000, from $55,000 to $29,000.

Simultaneous Death. A provision in the will may serve to defeat the *doctrine of commorientes.* According to this doctrine, if the order of death of two or more people in a common disaster cannot be established by evidence or logic, the younger will be deemed to have survived the elder. An exception exists when the younger person is a beneficiary under the other's will or life insurance policy.

Thus, if an intestate, childless couple is killed in an auto accident and the order of death is indeterminable with the husband being older than the wife, he will be deemed to have predeceased her and the bulk of his estate will be distributed among his wife's relatives. As a result, his estate will go where it was not intended and two sets of death duties will have to be paid. A will can prevent this from happening by providing that, if his wife predeceases him or survives him by no more than 30 days, any benefits to her from his will shall lapse.

Rates of Tax. The rate of federal Estate Tax levied is the same throughout Canada. The rate of Succession Duty varies in the provinces which impose it, namely British Columbia, Ontario and Quebec. In compensation, estates which have to pay provincial Succession Duty are granted substantial federal Estate Tax credits. The other provinces receive specified shares of the federal Estate Tax. Alberta receives 75%, which it

BENEFICIARY	NET AGGREGATE VALUE OF ESTATE	ALBERTA	BRITISH COLUMBIA	ONTARIO	QUEBEC	OTHER PROVINCES
Widow only	$ 50,000	$ 0	$ 0	$ 0	$ 1,200	$ 0
	75,000	450	1,300	900	4,500	1,800
	100,000	1,600	4,800	7,000	11,100	6,200
	150,000	4,200	13,200	18,300	21,900	16,800
	200,000	7,200	24,000	30,600	34,300	28,600
	300,000	13,800	47,400	57,400	63,600	55,200
	500,000	29,100	108,300	125,300	135,700	116,300
Two adult children only	$ 50,000	$ 0	$ 0	$ 0	$ 1,200	$ 0
	75,000	1,300	2,700	5,700	6,200	5,300
	100,000	2,600	6,600	10,900	12,100	10,200
	150,000	5,400	15,400	23,600	23,100	21,400
	200,000	8,400	26,400	36,400	34,800	33,600
	300,000	15,200	50,200	63,200	61,900	60,800
	500,000	30,700	111,700	123,700	129,000	122,900

refunds to the estate, however. Saskatchewan appears to be on the verge of following the same procedure in connection with the 75% share it receives, so as to prevent a flight of capital from the province.

There are many small countries in the world (for example, Monaco, The Bahamas, The Channel Islands) with practically no income taxes and death duties for people domiciled there, as a frankly admitted inducement to wealthy people to go and settle in those tax havens.

The table on page 112 gives a sample of total federal and provincial death duties payable in the different provinces.

GIFTS

Another way of *avoiding* death duties (*avoiding* is legal as contrasted to *evading*) is by a program of gifts during the lifetime of the monied member of the family. While federal Estate Tax and British Columbia Succession Duty must be paid on certain gifts made within three years of the donor's death, and Succession Duty must be paid in Ontario and Quebec on gifts made within five years of his death, federal Gift Tax must be paid on gifts exceeding the exempt amounts set out as follows:

- An unlimited number of gifts, not exceeding $1,000 to any one person in one year.
- Unlimited gifts to non-profit charitable or educational institutions or any branch of the government in Canada.
- Gifts, even to one person, totalling $4,000 a year or, roughly, half the person's net annual income (that is, what is left of his taxable income after paying federal income taxes), whichever is the greater.

In addition, a person may make a once-in-a-lifetime gift to his spouse of a home, or a share of a home, to a value not exceeding $10,000. (*See* page 24.) He may make a similar gift to a child, of land which he will use for farming.

It is hardly necessary to issue the warning that such substantial gifts should be made only to completely trusted persons. (*See* page 21.)

The tax authorities will consider a gift to have been made genuinely only if it was actually transferred to the recipient and if there was no condition attached to the gift, such as a right to take it back.

The amount of Gift Tax ranges on a sliding scale from 10% on taxable gifts below $5,000; 15% on $50,000; 20% on $250,000; to 28% on taxable gifts over $1,000,000.

ESTATE PLANNING

Another way to avoid Income Taxes and death duties is to form a *family corporation* in some cases. The tax structure may make it more advantageous for this corporation to pay corporation tax and for the corporation shareholders to pay income tax on their corporation dividends, than for ordinary Income Taxes to be paid.

It is open to a husband and wife to carry on a business as partners and to show each partner's share of the profits in a separate Income Tax return. However, the tax authorities habitually examine such situations very critically and will disallow the resulting income tax advantages if they consider that this was not an enterprise tantamount to an "at arm's length transaction". This term indicates a transaction which is perfectly genuine and proper and which might have been entered into with a non-related stranger also.

All the above topics fall in the general field of *estate planning*. They have been introduced very briefly, since they are subjects on which detailed advice should be sought from specialist tax consultants, whether they be lawyers or accountants.

APPENDIX

DATED JULY 2 A.D. 1968.

ADAM SPOUSE

– and –

EVE SPOUSE

AGREEMENT

BARR, BROWN and SOFORTH
50 Gould Street
Toronto, Ontario

THIS AGREEMENT made in duplicate this 2nd day of July, 1968

BETWEEN:

ADAM SPOUSE, of the City of Toronto, in the County of York, Merchant,

hereinafter called the "Husband" which expression shall where the context so admits include his personal representative

OF THE ONE PART,

– and –

EVE SPOUSE, of the said City of Toronto, wife of the said Adam Spouse,

hereinafter called the "Wife"
OF THE OTHER PART.

WHEREAS unhappy differences have arisen between the Husband and the Wife and they have mutually agreed to live separate and apart from each other for the future and are now living separate and apart and have mutually agreed to enter into the arrangements hereinafter expressed.

AND WHEREAS the Husband and the Wife were married at the City of Toronto, in the County of York on the 1st day of June, 1946.

AND WHEREAS the Husband and the Wife have three children namely, Thomas Spouse, born the 15th day of December, 1946, Richard Spouse, born the 18th day of September, 1950, and Henry Spouse, born the 1st day of October, 1953.

NOW THEREFORE THIS AGREEMENT WITNESSETH as follows: That in consideration of the premises and the covenants hereinafter expressed and contained and in pursuance of the said agreement the Husband and the Wife do covenant undertake and agree the one with the other:

1. The Husband and the Wife will henceforth live separate and apart from each other as if they were sole and unmarried and neither of them will molest or disturb or annoy or interfere with the other in any manner whatsoever and neither of them will take or cause to be taken any proceedings against the other of them for any cause or matter whatsoever arising out of or in any way connected with their marriage; provided that nothing herein contained shall constitute a bar to any proceedings which may be taken by either the Husband or the Wife for dissolution of their marriage or to enforce any of the terms of this agreement. The Wife shall be free from the control and authority of her Husband as if she were a feme sole and, subject to the provisions hereinafter contained respecting the place of residence of the child Henry Spouse, may reside at such place as she shall think fit.

2. Subject to the terms of this agreement, the Husband shall pay to the Wife for her support, maintenance and benefit so long as they both shall live the monthly sum of $300.00 payable on the first day of each and every month, the first of such payments to become due and payable on the first day of the month next following the execution of this agreement.

3. Notwithstanding the terms of paragraph 2 hereof, in the event that the circumstances of the Husband or of the Wife shall change after the making of this agreement having regard to the ability of the Husband to pay maintenance to the Wife and/or to the needs of the Wife to be maintained by the

Husband, then the quantum of the monthly payments payable by the Husband to the Wife for her support, maintenance and benefit may be varied by mutual agreement of the Husband and the Wife and in default of such agreement the quantum of the said monthly payments shall be varied to an amount to be determined by a single arbitrator to be chosen by the Husband and the Wife. This paragraph shall constitute a submission within the meaning of The Arbitration Act of Ontario. The terms of paragraph 2 hereof shall remain in full force and effect until the quantum of the said monthly payments is so varied by new agreement of the parties or by final award in such arbitration proceedings.

4. Notwithstanding anything herein contained all payments which the Husband is required to pay under the terms hereof for the benefit of the Wife shall be payable on condition that and only so long as the Wife continues to lead a chaste life and all such payments shall forthwith cease if the Wife shall at any time hereafter remarry in the event that the marriage of the Husband and the Wife is hereafter dissolved by a decree of a Court of competent jurisdiction.

5. The Wife shall have the sole custody, care and control of Henry Spouse the infant child of the Husband and the Wife provided that the Husband shall have access to the said child on 30 days of the year to be selected by him but no oftener than once a week including the right of the Husband to have the said child spend an uninterrupted period of 10 days with him during the month of July in each year and provided further that the Wife shall at no time have the child reside outside of the Province of Ontario or remove or cause to be removed the said child from the Province of Ontario without the written consent of the Husband.

6. The Husband shall pay to the Wife for the care, maintenance and support of the said child Henry Spouse the monthly sum of $100.00 payable on the first day of each and every month, the first of such payments to become due and payable on the first day of the month next following the execution of this agreement and such payments to be made so long as the said child while under the age of sixteen years continues to reside with the Wife and so long as the said child while over the age of sixteen years and under the age of twenty-one years continues to reside with the Wife and continues in regular attendance at a school, college or university whereof the Husband has given his approval in writing.

7. The Husband shall pay to the Wife for the care, main-

tenance and support of Richard Spouse the son of the Husband and the Wife the monthly sum of $100.00 payable on the first day of each and every month, the first of such payments to become due and payable on the first day of the month next following the execution of this agreement and such payments to be made so long as the said Richard Spouse while under the age of twenty-one years continues to reside with the Wife and continues in regular attendance at a school, college or university whereof the Husband has given his approval in writing.

8. The husband shall pay the proper tuition fees and other incidental fees properly payable to any school, college or university or schools, colleges or universities attended by the said Henry Spouse or the said Richard Spouse while respectively under the age of twenty-one years provided the Husband has given his approval thereof in writing.

9. The Husband shall forthwith deliver to the Wife the existing two policies of insurance on his life totalling in face value the amount of $60,000.00 namely:

> Policy #92800 of Cosmic Assurance Society
> having a face value of $30,000.00 and
> Policy #00829 of Diamond Insurance Company
> having a face value of $30,000.00,

and shall designate the Wife beneficiary thereof irrevocably under The Insurance Act of Ontario. The Husband shall maintain the said policies of insurance for the benefit of the Wife during her lifetime and shall pay the premium on each of the said policies of insurance as and when the same fall due until maturity of the said policies so that the said policies hereafter shall remain in full force and effect and the Wife shall remain beneficiary thereof without any change or revocation, provided that if the Wife does not lead a chaste life or if the marriage between the Husband and the Wife shall at any time hereafter be dissolved by the decree of a Court of competent jurisdiction and the Wife shall remarry or if the Wife shall predecease the Husband then upon the happening of any such event the Husband may deal with the said policies of insurance as he shall see fit and the Wife or her estate shall have no claim or interest therein and the Wife shall give any consents required to enable the Husband so to deal with the said policies. The Husband shall deliver to the Wife within two weeks next following the due date of the payment of each premium under each of the said policies of insurance a receipt covering payment in full of such premium and in default the Wife may pay such premium and recover the amount thereof from the Husband together with all costs and expenses incurred by her in so doing.

10. The Husband shall forthwith grant, transfer and convey to the wife all his interests in the lands and premises known as 1711 Greenvillage Avenue, in the said City of Toronto now owned by the Husband and the Wife as joint tenants subject to a mortgage in favour of the Temple Mortgage Corporation and the Wife shall pay all payments of the principal and interest on the said mortgage as and when the same fall due and shall keep the Husband indemnified against all monies which hereafter become due under the said mortgage and will save the Husband harmless from all liability thereunder and the Wife shall pay all municipal taxes and other charges which are levied and become due and payable in respect of the said lands and premises.

11. The Wife shall be absolutely entitled to all her clothing, jewellery and personal effects and all furniture, furnishings, fixtures, equipment, silverware and household effects now in or about the said premises, 1711 Greenvillage Avenue in the said City of Toronto and the Husband releases and quit claims unto the Wife any right or title which he has or may have therein.

12. The Wife shall not incur any debt or liability on the credit of the Husband and the Wife shall pay her own debts and will at all times hereafter keep indemnified the Husband from all torts, contracts, debts and liabilities committed, made, contracted or incurred by her under this agreement or otherwise and from all actions, proceedings, claims, demands, costs, damages and expenses whatsoever in respect of such debts or liabilities or any of them. If the Husband shall at any time or times hereafter be called on to pay or discharge and shall in fact pay or discharge any such debt or liability contracted or incurred by the Wife then and in any such case the Husband may at his option deduct and retain the amount which he has so paid out of any monies then due or thereafter to become due to the Wife under the terms of this agreement; provided that the Husband shall not pay any such debt or liability without first notifying the Wife of the existence thereof and giving her an opportunity to pay or dispute the same.

13. The Husband and the Wife and each of them accept the terms of this agreement in full and final satisfaction and dis-

charge of all claims and demands of every nature and kind whatsoever which one of them has or hereafter can, shall or may have against the other of them excepting always any claim arising under this agreement and in particular the Wife does hereby remise, release and forever discharge the Husband, his heirs, executors and administrators of and from all and any claims and demands for support, maintenance, alimony, interim alimony or any other claim of any nature or kind arising out of the marriage of the Husband and the Wife, and the Wife shall not at any time hereafter commence or prosecute any action or other proceedings for the recovery of support, maintenance, alimony or interim alimony from the Husband, provided always that nothing herein contained shall constitute a bar to any action or proceeding by either the Husband or the Wife against the other of them to enforce any of the terms of this agreement.

14. The Wife renounces all rights which she may have to the administration of the Husband's estate in the event of the Husband predeceasing her and renounces and releases the Husband from any claims which she may hereafter have against his estate for a distributive or preferential share under the Ontario Devolution of Estates Act or against his estate under the Ontario Dependants' Relief Act or any other statutes and any amendments thereto whereby a wife is or may be given a statutory claim against the estate of her husband.

15. The Husband renounces all rights which he may have to the administration of the Wife's estate in the event of the Wife predeceasing him and renounces and releases the Wife from any claims which he may hereafter have against her estate for a distributive or preferential share under the said Devolution of Estates Act or against her estate under the said Dependants' Relief Act or any other statutes and any amendments thereto whereby a husband is or may be given a statutory claim against the estate of his wife.

16. The Wife shall execute all such assurances or other instruments as may be necessary in order that any lands or any real property now owned by the Husband or hereafter acquired by him can be sold and conveyed by the Husband or his heirs, executors or administrators in the same manner as if he had never been married, and the Wife hereby irrevocably appoints the Husband her attorney for her and in her name to make and execute every deed, transfer, mortgage, charge or other instrument which may be necessary to bar her dower or inchoate right of dower, either legal or equitable,

or to grant, convey or discharge her interest in any lands or real property of any nature or kind, wheresoever situate which the Husband now owns or may hereafter acquire, and the Wife shall execute such further or other powers of attorney for all or any of the above purposes as the Husband may reasonably require, provided that nothing in this paragraph contained shall alter or derogate from the Husband's agreement herein contained to convey to the Wife the lands and premises known as 1711 Greenvillage Avenue, Toronto.

17. In the event that the Wife shall become bankrupt, or shall assign, charge or encumber the payments payable to her under the terms of this agreement or any part thereof, or do or suffer any act or thing whereby the said payments or some part thereof would, through her act of default or by operation or process of law, if belonging absolutely to her, become vested in or become payable to some other person or persons, then upon the occurring of any such event, and so long as the effect and operation thereof shall continue, her right to receive all payments hereunder shall cease and the said payments shall no longer be payable to her, and so until the cause for the said payments ceasing to be payable to her shall have ceased to exist or to be effectual or operate and then her right to receive the said payments shall revive and the said payments shall thereafter be payable to her as aforesaid unless or until the like event or any such event as aforesaid shall happen again whereby the said payments or some part thereof would, if belonging absolutely to her, become vested in or payable to some other person or persons, whereupon her right to receive such payments shall again cease and the said payments shall no longer be payable to her until the cause for the said payments ceasing to be payable to her shall have ceased to exist or be effectual or operate in the manner or to the like effect as above mentioned, and then her right to receive the said payments shall revive and they shall be payable to her as aforesaid, and so from time to time if and whensoever any of such events shall occur and the effect and operation thereof continue or discontinue as aforesaid. If any such event occurs as above mentioned in consequence of which the said payment shall not be payable to the Wife, then so long as the right of the Wife to receive the same shall have ceased and be not existing, the Husband or his personal representative may in his uncontrolled discretion expend such part thereof, if any, as he may deem advisable in and towards the maintenance of the Wife and/or of the children of the

Husband and the Wife for such purposes and on such conditions as he may think proper.

18. If at any future time the Husband and the Wife, with their mutual consent, cohabit as husband and wife for a continuous period of not less than 100 days, the payments payable to the Wife under the foregoing terms of this agreement shall thereupon cease to be payable and all the covenants, provisions and terms hereinbefore contained shall become void provided that nothing herein contained shall alter, affect, set aside, revoke or invalidate any payment, conveyance, act, matter or thing aforesaid made or done under and pursuant to the terms of this agreement.

19. The Husband and the Wife and each of them will from time to time and at all times hereafter upon every reasonable request and at the cost of the other of them execute and do all further assurances and things for the purpose of giving full effect to the covenants, provisions and terms of this agreement.

20. This agreement and every covenant, provision and term herein contained shall enure to the benefit of and be binding upon the Husband and the Wife and each of them, and their respective heirs, executors, administrators and assigns.

IN WITNESS WHEREOF the Husband and the Wife have hereunto set their hands and seals the day and year first above written.

SIGNED, SEALED and DELIVERED
In the presence of

____

____

Registrar's File No. 19

In the Supreme Court of Ontario

Petitioner

and

Respondent(s)

Petition for Divorce

Dye & Durham Limited, 76 Richmond St. East, Toronto
Law and Commercial Stationers

Solicitor for Petitioner:

Registrar's File No. 19

In the Supreme Court of Ontario

Between

PETITIONER

and

RESPONDENT(S)

PETITION FOR DIVORCE

(To be completed according to Form 140 as the same appears in the Rules of Practice)

To this Honourable Court:

I hereby petition for a decree of divorce from the Respondent spouse (*and where applicable* and for an order for alimony, custody, maintenance or costs)

on the grounds and in the circumstances following:

1. GROUNDS:

A. My Petition is under the DIVORCE ACT (Canada), section , subsection (and section , subsection *as the case may be*)

B. The particulars of my grounds for divorce are: (*here set forth fully but concisely all the material facts relied on but not the evidence by which they may be proved;*

in a case under section 4, subsection (1), paragraph (c) set forth the last place of cohabitation, the circumstances in which cohabitation ceased, the date when and the place where the respondent spouse was last seen or heard of and the steps taken to trace him)

2. RECONCILIATION:

A. The particulars of the circumstances which may assist the Court in ascertaining whether there is a possibility of reconciliation or resumption of cohabitation are:

(State "no efforts to reconcile have been made" if such be the case.)

B. (*where applicable*) The following efforts to reconcile have been made:

3. PARTICULARS OF MARRIAGE:

(Where possible, set out the particulars from the marriage certificate to be produced at the hearing)

A. The date of the marriage was:

B. The place of the marriage was:

C. The surname of the wife before marriage was:

D. The maiden surname of the wife was:

E. The marital status of the spouses at the time of the marriage was,
wife: husband:

F. The wife was born at
(province or country)
on 19
(month, day)

G. The husband was born at
(province or country)
on 19
(month, day)

4. DOMICILE AND JURISDICTION:

A. My residence is:

B. My spouse's residence is:

C. I ceased to cohabit with my spouse on or about:

D. My domicile is:

E. Such domicile has subsisted since:

F. I have (*or* The Respondent spouse has *as the case may be*) been ordinarily resident in Ontario since , 19 and actually resided in the said Province for months of that period at: (*set out place or places of residence*)

5. AGE AND DISABILITY:

(State "No party to these proceedings is under 21 years of age" if such be the case.)

A. The names of any of the parties under 21 years of age and the ages of such parties are:

(State "No party to these proceedings is under any other legal disability" if such be the case.)

B. The names of the parties suffering any other legal disability and the nature thereof are:

6. CHILDREN:

(State "there are no such children of the marriage" if such be the case.)

A. The names and dates of birth of all living children of the marriage as defined by the DIVORCE ACT (Canada) are:

(State "not applicable" where no children are shown in para. A.)

B. The particulars of the past, present and proposed custody, care, upbringing and education of the said child(ren) are as follows:

(State "not applicable" where no children are shown in para. A, or "no claim for custody is being made" if such be the case.)

C. I claim custody of the following child(ren):

(State "not applicable" if no claim for custody is being made.)

D. The facts on which such claim for custody is founded are:

7. OTHER PROCEEDINGS:

(State "there have been no such petitions or proceedings instituted" if such be the case.)

A. The particulars and status of all other petitions or proceedings instituted with reference to the marriage or any child thereof, including applications to the Parliament of Canada or actions for alimony or applications under any statute, are:

8. SEPARATION AGREEMENTS AND FINANCIAL ARRANGEMENTS:

(State "there have been no such written or oral agreements between the parties" if such be the case.)

A. The dates of any written or oral separation or financial agreements between the parties are:

(Complete where a claim for corollary relief is made or state "not applicable" if no such claim is made.)

B. (*where a claim for corollary relief is made*) The financial position, both income and capital, of the respective spouses is:

9. COLLUSION, CONDONATION AND CONNIVANCE:

A. There has been no collusion in relation to this Petition.

B. [*where the petition is under section 3 of the Divorce Act (Canada)*] There has been no condonation of or connivance at the grounds for divorce set forth in this Petition. (*or, where there has been either connivance or condonation give the full particulars of the facts on which the Court will be asked to find that the public interest would be better served by granting the decree*)

10. RELIEF ASKED:

I therefore ask this Honourable Court for the following relief:

A. A decree that I be divorced from the respondent, ...

B.

C.

etc., etc.

11. DECLARATION OF PETITIONER:

I have read and understand this Petition. Those statements contained therein of which

I have personal knowledge are true, and those of which I do not have personal knowledge I believe to be true.

DATED at , this day of , 19

....

....
(signature of petitioner)

....
(address of petitioner)

PLACE OF HEARING

I propose that this Petition be heard at the sittings of this Court at

STATEMENT OF SOLICITOR

I, the solicitor for , the Petitioner herein certify to this Court that I have complied with the requirements of section 7 of the DIVORCE ACT (Canada). *(Where the circumstances of the case are of such a nature that it would clearly not be appropriate to so comply, set out such circumstances)*

DATED at , this day of , 19

....
(signature of solicitor)

Registrar's File No. 19

In the Supreme Court of Ontario

Petitioner

and

Respondent(s)

Notice of Petition for Divorce

Dye & Durham Limited, 76 Richmond St. East, Toronto
Law and Commercial Stationers

Solicitor for Petitioner:

Registrar's File No. 19

In the Supreme Court of Ontario

Between

PETITIONER

(seal)

and

RESPONDENT(S)

NOTICE OF PETITION FOR DIVORCE

To of the (City) of ....

in the (County) of ....

And to: of the (City) of ....

in the (County) of ....

Take Notice that a Petition for a Decree of Divorce has been presented to this Court by the Petitioner. A copy of it is attached to this notice.

And Further Take Notice that if you wish to oppose the said Petition or if you wish other relief you must cause your Answer to be served on the Petitioner and filed with proof of service in the office of the undersigned registrar within the time hereinafter stated:

Where you are served within Ontario, within twenty days after service on you of this Notice, inclusive of the day of such service;

Where you are served elsewhere in Canada or within one of the United States of America, within forty days after service on you of this Notice, inclusive of the day of such service; or

Where you are served elsewhere than within Canada or within one of the United States of America, within days after service on you of this Notice, inclusive of the day of such service, as provided in the order of the Court authorizing such service to be made.

And Further Take Notice that in default of your serving and filing such Answer within the time prescribed above the Petitioner may proceed herein and (subject to the Rules of Court) you will not be entitled to notice of any further proceedings and a decree and other relief may be given in your absence.

And Further Take Notice that in default of Answer this proceeding may be set down within thirty days of such default for hearing at the sittings of this Court at
and where so set down and subject to the Rules of Court, you will not be entitled to any further notice of the hearing.

And Further Take Notice that you may ascertain the approximate date of the hearing of the said Petition and the date and details of any decree from the office of the said registrar.

And Further Take Notice that any decree given at such hearing may become final after the expiration of such time from the granting thereof as the decree may provide unless in the meantime you deliver to the undersigned and to the Petitioner and to Her Majesty's Proctor at Toronto, a written Notice that you wish to show cause why the decree should not become final and the grounds therefor.

And Further Take Notice that neither spouse is free to remarry as a result of these proceedings until a decree of divorce has been granted and such decree has been made final.

DATED at , the day of , 19

....

Registrar, S.C.O.

....

(full address)

....

The Petitioner's address is: ....

....

This Notice of Petition was issued on behalf of the Petitioner by: solicitor(s)

whose address is:

NOTE 1: This Notice is to be served upon the respondent spouse within sixty days from the date on which it was issued, unless otherwise ordered.

NOTE 2: The person who serves this notice shall at the time of service request each respondent to complete and sign in his presence the following form of acknowledgment of service and shall sign his name as a witness to any signature thereto.

I am the person named as
a Respondent in this Notice of Petition. I have this day received a copy of the within Notice and attached Petition and my mailing address for further service of documents is

....

....

WITNESS

....
(signature)

I am the person named as
a Respondent in this Notice of Petition. I have this day received a copy of the within Notice and attached Petition and my mailing address for further service of documents is

....

....

WITNESS

....
(signature)

16 ELIZABETH II

CHAP. 24

An Act respecting Divorce

[Assented to 1 February, 1968]

Her Majesty, by and with the advice and consent of the Senate and House of Commons of Canada, enacts as follows:

SHORT TITLE

1. This Act may be cited as the *Divorce Act*. **Short title**

INTERPRETATION

2. In this Act,

Definitions

(*a*) "child" of a husband and wife includes any person to whom the husband and wife stand *in loco parentis* and any person of whom either of the husband or the wife is a parent and to whom the other of them stands *in loco parentis;* **"Child"**

(*b*) "children of the marriage" means each child of a husband and wife who at the material time is **"Children of the marriage"**

(i) under the age of sixteen years, or

(ii) sixteen years of age or over and under their charge but unable, by reason of illness, disability or other cause, to withdraw himself from their charge or to provide himself with necessaries of life;

(*c*) "collusion" means an agreement or conspiracy to which a petitioner is either directly or indirectly a party for the purpose of subverting the administration of justice, and includes any agreement, understanding or arrangement to fabricate or suppress evidence or to deceive the court, but does not include an agreement to the **"Collusion"** extent that it provides for separation between the parties, financial support, division of property interests or the custody, care or upbringing of children of the marriage;

"Condonation"

(*d*) "condonation" does not include the continuation or resumption of cohabitation during any single period of not more than ninety days, where such cohabitation is continued or resumed with reconciliation as its primary purpose;

"Court"

(*e*) "court" for any province means,

(i) for the Province of Ontario, Nova Scotia, New Brunswick or Alberta, the trial division or branch of the Supreme Court of the Province,

(ii) for the Province of Quebec,

(A) where no proclamation has been issued under subsection (1) of section 22, the Divorce Division of the Exchequer Court, or

(B) where a proclamation has been issued under subsection (1) of section 22, the Superior Court of the Province,

(iii) for the Province of Newfoundland,

(A) where no proclamation has been issued under subsection (2) of section 22, the Divorce Division of the Exchequer Court, or

(B) where a proclamation has been issued under subsection (2) of section 22, the Supreme Court of the Province,

(iv) for the Province of British Columbia or Prince Edward Island, the Supreme Court of the Province,

(v) for the Province of Manitoba or Saskatchewan, the Court of Queen's Bench for the Province, and

(vi) for the Yukon Territory or the Northwest Territories, the Territorial Court thereof;

(*f*) "court of appeal" means **"Court of appeal"**

(i) with respect to an appeal from a court other than the Divorce Division of the Exchequer Court, the court exercising general appellate jurisdiction with respect to appeals from that court, and

(ii) with respect to an appeal from the Divorce Division of the Exchequer Court, the Exchequer Court of Canada; and

(*g*) "petition" for divorce means a petition or motion for a decree of divorce, either with or without corollary relief by way of an order under section 10 or 11. **"Petition"**

GROUNDS FOR DIVORCE

3. Subject to section 5, a petition for divorce may be presented to a court by a husband or wife, on the ground that the respondent, since the celebration of the marriage, **Grounds**

(*a*) has committed adultery;

(*b*) has been guilty of sodomy, bestiality or rape, or has engaged in a homosexual act;

(*c*) has gone through a form of marriage with another person; or

(*d*) has treated the petitioner with physical or mental cruelty of such a kind as to render intolerable the continued cohabitation of the spouses.

Additional grounds

4. (1) In addition to the grounds specified in section 3, and subject to section 5, a petition for divorce may be presented to a court by a husband or wife where the husband and wife are living separate and apart, on the ground that there has been a permanent breakdown of their marriage by reason of one or more of the following circumstances as specified in the petition, namely:

(*a*) the respondent

(i) has been imprisoned, pursuant to his conviction for one or more offences, for a period or an aggregate period of not less than three years during the five-year period immediately preceding the presentation of the petition, or

(ii) has been imprisoned for a period of not less than two years immediately preceding the presentation of the petition pursuant to his conviction for an offence for which he was sentenced to death or to imprisonment for a term of ten years or more, against which conviction or sentence all rights of the respondent to appeal to a court having jurisdiction to hear such an appeal have been exhausted;

(*b*) the respondent has, for a period of not less than three years immediately preceding the presentation of the petition, been grossly addicted to alcohol, or a narcotic as defined in the *Narcotic Control Act*, and there is no reasonable expectation of the respondent's rehabilitation within a reasonably foreseeable period;

(*c*) the petitioner, for a period of not less than three years immediately preceding the presentation of the petition, has had no knowledge of or information as to the whereabouts of the respondent and, throughout that period, has been unable to locate the respondent;

(*d*) the marriage has not been consummated and the respondent, for a period of not less than one year, has been unable by reason of illness or disability to consummate the marriage, or has refused to consummate it; or

(*e*) the spouses have been living separate and apart

(i) for any reason other than that described in subparagraph (ii), for a period of not less than three years, or

(ii) by reason of the petitioner's desertion of the respondent, for a period of not less than five years,

immediately preceding the presentation of the petition.

Where circumstances established

(2) On any petition presented under this section, where the existence of any of the circumstances described in subsection (1) has been established, a permanent breakdown of the marriage by reason of those circumstances shall be deemed to have been established.

Jurisdiction of Court

Jurisdiction to entertain petition

5. (1) The court for any province has jurisdiction to entertain a petition for divorce and to grant relief in respect thereof if,

(*a*) the petition is presented by a person domiciled in Canada; and

(*b*) either the petitioner or the respondent has been ordinarily resident in that province for a period of at least one year immediately preceding the presentation of the petition and has actually resided in that province for at least ten months of that period.

Where petition pending before two courts

(2) Where petitions for divorce are pending between a husband and wife before each of two courts that would otherwise have jurisdiction under this Act respectively to entertain them and to grant relief in respect thereof,

(*a*) if the petitions were presented on different days and the petition that was presented first is not discontinued within thirty days after the day it was presented, the court to which a petition was first presented has exclusive jurisdiction to grant relief between the parties and the other petition shall be deemed to be discontinued; and

(*b*) if the petitions were presented on the same day and neither of them is discontinued within thirty days after that day, the Divorce Division of the Exchequer Court has exclusive jurisdiction to grant relief between the parties and the petition or petitions pending before the other court or courts shall be removed, by direction of the Divorce Division of the Exchequer Court, into that Court for adjudication.

Where petition opposed

(3) Where a husband or wife opposes a petition for divorce, the court may grant to such spouse the relief that might have been granted to him or to her if he or she had presented a petition to the court seeking that relief and the court had had jurisdiction to entertain the petition under this Act.

Domicile

Rule for determining domicile

6. (1) For all purposes of establishing the jurisdiction of a court to grant a decree of divorce under this Act, the domicile of a married woman shall be determined as if she were unmarried and, if she is a minor, as if she had attained her majority.

Recognition of foreign decrees based on wife's domicile

(2) For all purposes of determining the marital status in Canada of any person and without limiting or restricting any existing rule of law applicable to the recognition of decrees of divorce granted otherwise than under this Act, recognition shall be given to a decree of divorce, granted after the coming into force of this Act under a law of a country or subdivision of a country other than Canada by a tribunal or other competent authority that had jurisdiction under that law to grant the decree, on the basis of the domicile of the wife in that country or subdivision determined as if she were unmarried and, if she was a minor, as if she had attained her majority.

Presentation and Hearing of Petitions:

Special Duties

Duty of legal adviser respecting possibility of reconciliation

7. (1) It shall be the duty of every barrister, solicitor, lawyer or advocate who undertakes to act on behalf of a petitioner or a respondent on a petition for divorce under this Act, except where the circumstances of the case are of such a nature that it would clearly not be appropriate to do so,

(*a*) to draw to the attention of his client those provisions of this Act that have as their object the effecting where possible of the reconciliation of the parties to a marriage;

(*b*) to inform his client of the marriage counselling or guidance facilities known to him that might endeavour to assist the client and his or her spouse with a view to their possible reconciliation; and

(*c*) to discuss with his client the possibility of the client's reconciliation with his or her spouse.

Statement to be endorsed on petition

(2) Every petition for divorce that is presented to a court by a barrister, solicitor, lawyer or advocate on behalf of a petitioner shall have endorsed thereon a statement by such barrister, solicitor, lawyer or advocate certifying that he has complied with the requirements of this section.

Reconciliation proceedings

8. (1) On a petition for divorce it shall be the duty of the court, before proceeding to the hearing of the evidence, to direct such inquiries to the petitioner and, where the respondent is present, to the respondent as the court deems necessary in order to ascertain whether a possibility exists of their reconciliation, unless the circumstances of the case are of such a nature that it would clearly not be appropriate to do so, and if at that or any later stage in the proceedings it appears to the court from the nature of the case, the evidence or the attitude of the parties or either of them that there is a possibility of such a reconciliation, the court shall

(*a*) adjourn the proceedings to afford the parties an opportunity of becoming reconciled; and

(*b*) with the consent of the parties or in the discretion of the court, nominate

(i) a person with experience or training in marriage counselling or guidance, or

(ii) in special circumstances, some other suitable person,

to endeavour to assist the parties with a view to their possible reconciliation.

Resumption of hearing

(2) Where fourteen days have elapsed from the date of any adjournment under sub-

section (1) and either of the parties applies to the court to have the proceedings resumed, the court shall resume the proceedings.

ADDITIONAL DUTIES OF COURT

Duty of court on petition

9. (1) On a petition for divorce it shall be the duty of the court

(*a*) to refuse a decree based solely upon the consent, admissions or default of the parties or either of them, and not to grant a decree except after a trial which shall be by a judge, without a jury;

(*b*) to satisfy itself that there has been no collusion in relation to the petition and to dismiss the petition if it finds that there was collusion in presenting or prosecuting it;

(*c*) where a decree is sought under section 3, to satisfy itself that there has been no condonation or connivance on the part of the petitioner, and to dismiss the petition if the petitioner has condoned or connived at the act or conduct complained of unless, in the opinion of the court, the public interest would be better served by granting the decree;

(*d*) where a decree is sought under section 4, to refuse the decree if there is a reasonable expectation that cohabitation will occur or be resumed within a reasonably foreseeable period;

(*e*) where a decree is sought under section 4, to refuse the decree if there are children of the marriage and the granting of the decree would prejudicially affect the making of reasonable arrangements for their maintenance; and

(*f*) where a decree is sought under section 4 by reason of circumstances described in paragraph (*e*) of subsection (1) of that section, to refuse the decree if the granting of the decree would be unduly harsh or unjust to either spouse or would prejudicially affect the making of such reasonable arrangements for the maintenance of either spouse as are necessary in the circumstances.

Revival

(2) Any act or conduct that has been condoned is not capable of being revived so as to constitute a ground for divorce described in section 3.

Calculation of period of separation

(3) For the purposes of paragraph (*e*) of subsection (1) of section 4, a period during which a husband and wife have been living separate and apart shall not be considered to have been interrupted or terminated

(*a*) by reason only that either spouse has become incapable of forming or having an intention to continue to live so separate and apart or of continuing to live so separate and apart of his or her own volition, if it appears to the court that the separation would probably have continued if such spouse had not become so incapable; or

(*b*) by reason only that there has been a resumption of cohabitation by the spouses during a single period of not more than ninety days with reconciliation as its primary purpose.

Corollary Relief

Interim orders

10. Where a petition for divorce has been presented, the court having jurisdiction to grant relief in respect thereof may make such interim orders as it thinks fit and just

(*a*) for the payment of alimony or an

alimentary pension by either spouse for the maintenance of the other pending the hearing and determination of the petition, accordingly as the court thinks reasonable having regard to the means and needs of each of them;

(*b*) for the maintenance of and the custody, care and upbringing of the children of the marriage pending the hearing and determination of the petition; or

(*c*) for relieving either spouse of any subsisting obligation to cohabit with the other.

Orders granting corollary relief

11. (1) Upon granting a *decree nisi* of divorce, the court may, if it thinks it fit and just to do so having regard to the conduct of the parties and the condition, means and other circumstances of each of them, make one or more of the following orders, namely:

(*a*) an order requiring the husband to secure or to pay such lump sum or periodic sums as the court thinks reasonable for the maintenance of both or either

(i) the wife, and

(ii) the children of the marriage;

(*b*) an order requiring the wife to secure or to pay such lump sum or periodic sums as the court thinks reasonable for the maintenance of both or either

(i) the husband, and

(ii) the children of the marriage; and

(*c*) an order providing for the custody, care and upbringing of the children of the marriage.

Variation, etc., of order granting corollary relief

(2) An order made pursuant to this section may be varied from time to time or rescinded by the court that made the order if it thinks it fit and just to do so having regard to

the conduct of the parties since the making of the order or any change in the condition, means or other circumstances of either of them.

Payment and conditions

12. Where a court makes an order pursuant to section 10 or 11, it may

(*a*) direct that any alimony, alimentary pension or maintenance be paid either to the husband or wife, as the case may be, or to a trustee or administrator approved by the court; and

(*b*) impose such terms, conditions or restrictions as the court thinks fit and just.

Decrees and Orders

Decree nisi

13. (1) Every decree of divorce shall in the first instance be a *decree nisi* and no such decree shall be made absolute until three months have elapsed from the granting of the decree and the court is satisfied that every right to appeal from the judgment granting the decree has been exhausted.

Special circumstances

(2) Notwithstanding subsection (1), where, upon or after the granting of a *decree nisi* of divorce,

(*a*) the court is of opinion that by reason of special circumstances it would be in the public interest for the decree to be made absolute before the time when it could be made absolute under subsection (1), and

(*b*) the parties agree and undertake that no appeal will be taken, or any appeal that has been taken has been abandoned,

the court may fix a shorter time after which the decree may be made absolute or, in its discretion, may then make the decree absolute.

Cause may be shown

(3) Where a *decree nisi* of divorce has been granted but not made absolute, any per-

son may show cause to the court why the decree should not be made absolute, by reason of its having been obtained by collusion, by reason of the reconciliation of the parties or by reason of any other material facts, and in any such case the court may by order,

(*a*) rescind the *decree nisi*;

(*b*) require further inquiry to be made; or

(*c*) make such further order as the court thinks fit.

Where decree not made absolute

(4) Where a *decree nisi* of divorce has been granted by a court and no application has been made by the party to whom the decree was granted to have it made absolute, then, at any time after the expiration of one month from the earliest date on which that party could have made such an application, the party against whom it was granted may apply to the court to have the decree made absolute and, subject to any order made under subsection (3), the court may then make the decree absolute.

Effect of decree or order

14. A decree of divorce granted under this Act or an order made under section 10 or 11 has legal effect throughout Canada.

Registration and enforcement of orders

15. An order made under section 10 or 11 by any court may be registered in any other superior court in Canada and may be enforced in like manner as an order of that superior court or in such other manner as is provided for by any rules of court or regulations made under section 19.

Decree absolute

16. Where a decree of divorce has been made absolute under this Act, either party to the former marriage may marry again.

APPEALS

Appeal to court of appeal

17. (1) Subject to subsection (3), an appeal lies to the court of appeal from a judgment or

order, whether final or interlocutory, other than a decree absolute, pronounced by a court under this Act.

Powers of court of appeal

(2) The court of appeal may

(*a*) dismiss the appeal; or

(*b*) allow the appeal and

(i) pronounce the judgment that ought to have been pronounced including such order or such further or other order as it deems just, or

(ii) order a new trial where it deems it necessary to do so to correct a substantial wrong or miscarriage of justice.

Notice of appeal

(3) An appeal under subsection (1) shall be brought by filing a notice of appeal in the court of appeal not later than fifteen days after the pronouncing of the judgment or the making of the order being appealed from.

Extension of time

(4) Except where a decree of divorce has been made absolute, the court of appeal or a judge thereof may, on special grounds, either before or after the expiration of the time fixed by subsection (3) for bringing an appeal, by order extend that time.

Appeal to Supreme Court of Canada

18. (1) An appeal lies on a question of law to the Supreme Court of Canada with leave of that court from a decision of the court of appeal under section 17.

Leave to Appeal

(2) Leave to appeal under this section may be granted within thirty days from the pronouncing of the judgment or order being appealed from or within such extended time as the Supreme Court of Canada or a judge thereof may, before the expiration of those thirty days, fix or allow.

RULES OF COURT

19. (1) A court or court of appeal may make rules of court applicable to any proceedings under this Act within the jurisdiction of that court, including, without restricting the generality of the foregoing, rules of court

Rules of court

(*a*) regulating the pleading, practice and procedure in the court, including the addition of persons as parties to the proceedings;

(*b*) regulating the sittings of the court;

(*c*) respecting the fixing and awarding of costs;

(*d*) providing for the registration and enforcement of orders made under this Act including their enforcement after death; and

(*e*) prescribing and regulating the duties of officers of the court and any other matter considered expedient to attain the ends of justice and carry into effect the purposes and provisions of this Act.

(2) Notwithstanding subsection (1), the Governor in Council may make such regulations as he considers proper to assure uniformity in the rules of court made under this Act, and any regulations made under this subsection prevail over rules of court made under subsection (1).

Regulations

(3) The provisions of any law or of any rule of court, regulation or other instrument made thereunder respecting any matter in relation to which rules of court may be made under subsection (1), that were in force in Canada or any province immediately before the coming into force of this Act and that are not inconsistent with this Act, continue in force as though enacted or made by or under this Act until such time as they are altered by rules of

Continuation of procedural laws

court or regulations made under this section or are, by virtue of the making of any rules of court or regulations under this section, rendered inconsistent with those rules or regulations.

EVIDENCE

Provincial laws of evidence

20. (1) Subject to this or any other Act of the Parliament of Canada, the laws of evidence of the province in which any proceedings under this Act are taken, including the laws of proof of service of any petition or other document, apply to such proceedings.

Where proceedings deemed taken

(2) For the purposes of this section,

(*a*) where any proceedings under this Act are taken before the Divorce Division of the Exchequer Court as the court for any province, the proceedings shall be deemed to be taken in that proince; and

(b) where any petitions for divorce pending between a husband and wife are removed under subsection (2) of section 5 by direction of the Divorce Division of the Exchequer Court into that Court for adjudication, the proceedings shall be deemed to be taken in the province specified in such direction to be the province with which the husband and wife are or have been most closely associated according to the facts appearing from the petitions.

Admissions and communications made in course of reconciliation proceedings

21. (1) A person nominated by a court under this Act to endeavour to assist the parties to a marriage with a view to their possible reconciliation is not competent or compellable in any legal proceedings to disclose any admission or communication made to him in his capacity as the nominee of the court for that purpose.

Idem

(2) Evidence of anything said or of any

admission or communication made in the course of an endeavour to assist the parties to a marriage with a view to their possible reconciliation is not admissible in any legal proceedings.

QUEBEC AND NEWFOUNDLAND COURTS

22. (1) The Governor in Council may, on the recommendation of the Lieutenant Governor in Council of Quebec, issue a proclamation declaring the Superior Court of Quebec to be the court for that Province for the purposes of this Act, and on or after the issue of such proclamation any petition for divorce presented under section 3 or 4 that would, if it had been presented after the coming into force of this Act but before the issue of the proclamation, have been presented to the Divorce Division of the Exchequer Court as the court for that Province, shall be presented to the Superior Court of Quebec.

Proclamation respecting Superior Court of Quebec

(2) The Governor in Council may, on the recommendation of the Lieutenant Governor in Council of Newfoundland, issue a proclamation declaring the Supreme Court of Newfoundland to be the court for that Province for the purposes of this Act, and on or after the issue of such proclamation any petition for divorce presented under section 3 or 4 that would, if it had been presented after the coming into force of this Act but before the issue of the proclamation, have been presented to the Divorce Division of the Exchequer Court as the court for that Province, shall be presented to the Supreme Court of Newfoundland.

Proclamation respecting Supreme Court of Newfoundland

(3) Subject to subsection (4) but notwithstanding any other provision of this Act, where a proclamation has been issued under subsection (1) or (2) a petition for divorce presented to the Divorce Division of the Exchequer Court before the proclamation was issued shall be dealt with and disposed of as if the proclamation had not been issued.

Petition previously presented to Divorce Division of Exchequer Court

Variation of order made by Divorce Division of Exchequer Court

(4) Where a decree of divorce has been granted by the Divorce Division of the Exchequer Court

(*a*) after the coming into force of this Act but before the issue of a proclamation referred to in subsection (3), or

(*b*) pursuant to subsection (3),

any order made pursuant to subsection (1) of section 11 may be varied from time to time or rescinded pursuant to subsection (2) of that section by the court that would have had jurisdiction to grant the decree of divorce corollary to which the order was made if the proclamation had been issued at the time when the petition for the decree was presented and that court had made the order by way of corollary relief in respect of a petition presented to it.

CONSEQUENTIAL AMENDMENTS

R.S., c. 98

23. (1) The *Exchequer Court Act* is amended by adding thereto, immediately after section 4 thereof, the following sections:

Divorce Division

"4A. (1) A division of the Exchequer Court called the Divorce Division is hereby established.

Constitution of Divorce Division

(2) The Divorce Division shall consist of the following regular judges:

(*a*) the judge of the Court who was designated under section 6A to exercise and perform the powers, duties and functions of the officer of the Senate referred to in section 3 of the *Dissolution and Annulment of Marriages Act*, and

(*b*) such other judges of the Court as may, in the instruments authorizing their appointment, be designated as judges of the Divorce Division.

Ex officio judges

(3) Notwithstanding subsection (2), the President of the Court is *ex officio* Presi-

dent of the Divorce Division and each of the puisne judges is *ex officio* a judge of the Divorce Division, and as such have and may exercise in all respects, the same jurisdiction as regular judges of the Divorce Division.

Registrar

(4) The Registrar of the Court is *ex officio* the Registrar of the Divorce Division.

Sittings

4B. Subject to the rules of court and except as otherwise provided by any order made by the Governor in Council, any judge of the Divorce Division may sit and act at any time and at any place in Canada for the transaction of the business of the Divorce Division or any part thereof."

(2) Section 8 of the said Act is repealed and the following substituted therefor:

Persons qualified to sit and act as judge

"8. (1) Subject to subsection (3) any judge of a superior court or county court in Canada, and any person who has held office as a judge of a superior court or county court in Canada, may, at the request of the President made with the approval of the Governor in Council, sit and act as a judge of the Exchequer Court and as a judge of the Divorce Division.

Consent of Attorney General

(2) No request may be made under subsection (1) to a judge of a provincial court without the consent of the Attorney General of that province.

Approval of Governor in Council

(3) The Governor in Council may approve the making of requests pursuant to subsection (1) either specifically or in general terms, and for particular periods or purposes, and in approving in general terms any such request may limit the number of persons who may sit and act pursuant to any request.

Remuneration while acting

(4) A person who sits and acts as a judge pursuant to subsection (1) shall be

paid a salary for the period he so sits and acts at the rate fixed by the *Judges Act* for puisne judges of the Exchequer Court less any amount otherwise payable to him under that Act in respect of that period."

(3) Section 33 of the said Act is amended by adding thereto the following subsection:

Quorum for appeals under *Divorce Act*

"(2) Notwithstanding subsection (1), not less than three judges of the Exchequer Court shall sit and act on the hearing and determination of any appeal to the Exchequer Court under section 17 of the *Divorce Act*, but in no case shall a judge who has heard a petition for divorce sit and act on the hearing and determination of any appeal under that section from a judgment or order in respect of that petition."

R.S., c. 176

24. (1) The long title to the *Marriage and Divorce Act* is repealed and the following substituted therefor:

"An Act respecting Marriage"

(2) Section 1 of the said Act is repealed and the following substituted therefor:

Short title

"1. This Act may be cited as the *Marriage Act*."

(3) The heading preceding section 4 and sections 4 to 6 of the said Act are repealed.

TRANSITIONAL AND REPEAL

Petition presented after commencement of Act

25. (1) A petition for divorce presented in Canada after the coming into force of this Act shall be governed and regulated by this Act, whether or not the material facts or circumstances giving rise to the petition occurred wholly or partly before the coming into force of this Act.

Where proceedings or petition previously commenced

(2) Notwithstanding the repeal by section 26 of the Acts and laws referred to in that section but subject to subsection (3) of this section,

(*a*) any proceedings for divorce commenced in any court in Canada of competent jurisdiction before the coming into force of this Act and not finally disposed of when this Act comes into force, shall be dealt with and disposed of in accordance with the law as it was immediately before the coming into force of this Act, as though that law had not been repealed; and

(*b*) any petition for the dissolution or annulment of a marriage filed under the *Dissolution and Annulment of Marriages Act* before the coming into force of this Act and not finally disposed of when this Act comes into force shall be dealt with and disposed of in accordance with that Act, as though that Act had not been repealed.

Variation of order previously made

(3) Where a decree of divorce has been granted before the coming into force of this Act or pursuant to subsection (2), any order to the effect described in subsection (1) of section 11 may be varied from time to time or rescinded in accordance with subsection (2) of that section by the court that would have had jurisdiction to grant the decree of divorce corollary to which the order was made if this Act had been in force at the time when the petition for the decree was presented and that court had made the order by way of corollary relief in respect of a petition presented to it.

Repeal

26. (1) The *Dissolution and Annulment of Marriages Act*, the *Divorce Jurisdiction Act*, the *Divorce Act (Ontario)*, in so far as it relates to the dissolution of marriage, and the *British Columbia Divorce Appeals Act* are repealed.

Idem

(2) Subject to subsection (3) of section 19, all other laws respecting divorce that were in force in Canada or any province immedi-

ately before the coming into force of this Act are repealed, but nothing in this Act shall be construed as repealing any such law to the extent that it constitutes authority for any other matrimonial cause.

COMMENCEMENT

Coming into force

27. This Act shall come into force on such day not earlier than three months after the date this Act is assented to as may be fixed by proclamation.

INDEX